MANAGEMENT CASE STUDIES: TACKLING REAL-WORLD CHALLENGES

DR. AMRITA BAID MORE
DR. MANPREET KAUR BHATIA
DR. ARPAN SHRIVASTAVA

Made with ♥ on the Notion Press Platform
www.notionpress.com

Contents

Contents

Contents

Contents

Contents

Preface

In the dynamic and ever-evolving management world, understanding real-world scenarios and applying theoretical concepts to practical situations has become essential for students, professionals, and academicians. Case studies serve as a bridge between theory and practice, providing a structured approach to analysing complex problems, developing strategic thinking, and honing decision-making skills. The book "**Management Case Studies: Tackling Real-World Challenges**" is a compilation of diverse cases across various domains of management, meticulously designed to enhance the learning experience and provide readers with a comprehensive understanding of contemporary business challenges.

The cases presented in this book cover a wide range of topics, including marketing, finance, human resource management, operations, strategy, and emerging areas such as sustainability and technology management. Each case is based on real-world scenarios, reflecting the complexities of today's global business environment. The cases encourage critical thinking, creativity, and collaboration by placing readers in the decision-makers role, where they must analyze situations, identify problems, evaluate alternatives, and propose actionable solutions.

This book is structured to cater to a broad audience, from management students and educators to industry professionals. For students, the cases provide an opportunity to apply classroom learning to practical situations, fostering a deeper understanding of management concepts. For educators, the cases serve as a valuable resource for stimulating classroom discussions and engaging students in active learning. For professionals, the cases offer insights into strategic decision-making and problem-solving, helping them navigate the challenges of their respective industries.

The objective of this book is not only to present challenges faced by organizations but also to inspire innovative thinking and strategic foresight. Each case is accompanied by thought-provoking questions that encourage readers to delve deeper into the issues at hand, analyze from multiple perspectives, and derive meaningful conclusions. These questions are designed to stimulate discussions and debates, fostering a collaborative learning environment.

A significant focus of this book is on relevance and applicability. The cases span industries, geographies, and organizational sizes, ensuring that readers gain a holistic perspective on management practices. From multinational corporations to startups, from traditional industries to disruptive innovators, the cases reflect the diverse spectrum of management challenges in the modern world.

In curating this collection, we have drawn upon extensive research, industry insights, and academic expertise to ensure that each case is engaging, informative, and impactful. The emphasis has been on creating content that is not only academically rigorous but also practically relevant, bridging the gap between theoretical learning and real-world application.

We are confident that this book will serve as a valuable companion in your journey of exploring the multifaceted world of management. We hope that these case studies will not only enhance your understanding of management principles but also inspire you to think critically, act decisively, and contribute meaningfully to the organizations and communities you serve.

We extend our gratitude to all the contributors, researchers, and industry experts whose efforts have enriched this book. We also thank the readers for choosing this resource, and we welcome your feedback and suggestions for future editions. Together, let us embark on this journey of learning, exploration, and growth.

Dr. Amrita Baid More
Dr. Manpreet Kaur Bhatia
& Dr. Arpan Shrivastava
Author

Acknowledgements

I would like to thank my supervisor, Professo[r]
[...]ous encouragement and support from the ve[ry]
being a very busy man [...]

Author Acknowledgment – (i)

With a heart full of gratitude, I humbly acknowledge the unwavering support and love of those who have been instrumental in shaping me and my journey toward this milestone.

First and foremost, I bow in reverence to my parents, whose endless sacrifices, blessings, and belief in my abilities laid the foundation of my aspirations. Their love and values continue to guide me at every step of my life.

To my husband, my anchor and greatest source of strength, thank you for your patience, encouragement, and unwavering faith in my dreams. Your partnership and understanding have been the wind beneath my wings.

To my son, the light of my life, your innocent smiles and boundless love inspire me to strive harder and become a better version of myself every day.

To my extended family, whose silent yet significant presence has always been a source of strength, I am forever grateful for your encouragement and prayers.

I also wish to express my heartfelt thanks to all the people I have crossed paths with, each of whom has contributed, in one way or another, to making me who I am today. Teachers, mentors, colleagues, friends, and even fleeting acquaintances have all enriched my journey with their wisdom, kindness, and experiences.

Finally, I dedicate this work to all those who believed in me, often more than I believed in myself. It is because of your love and support that this book has been made possible.

Thank you from the depths of my heart.

Dr. Amrita Baid More
Author

Author Acknowledgement – (ii)

I am profoundly grateful to everyone who has supported and encouraged me in successfully completing this book.

First and foremost, I express my heartfelt gratitude to the Almighty for His countless blessings, guidance, and strength, which have been my constant source of inspiration throughout this journey.

I owe a deep sense of gratitude to my parents for their unwavering encouragement, endless patience, and unwavering belief in my endeavors. Their love and support have been the cornerstone of my achievements.

I would like to extend my sincere thanks to the leadership at Medicaps University, including our esteemed Chancellor, Shri R. C. Mittal; Honorable Vice-Chancellor, Prof. (Dr.) Dilip K. Patnaik; OSD to Chancellor, Shri Palash Garg; Director Branding, Ms. Saloni Garg; Pro Vice-Chancellor, Prof. (Dr.) D. K. Panda; Dean of the Faculty of Management Studies, Prof. (Dr.) Sanjay Jain; and HOD, Prof. (Dr.) Kalyan Sahoo. Their guidance, encouragement, and support have been instrumental in shaping this work.

I am also deeply thankful to my mentors, colleagues, and peers for their valuable insights and constructive feedback, which have enriched the quality of this book.

Lastly, I extend my gratitude to my students and readers, whose curiosity, enthusiasm, and dedication to learning have been a constant source of motivation for me. This book is a tribute to the pursuit of knowledge and the enduring spirit of lifelong learning.

Thank you all for being an integral part of this meaningful journey.

Dr. Manpreet Kaur Bhatia
Author

Author Acknowledgement – (iii)

I am deeply grateful to everyone who has supported me in completing this book successfully. First and foremost, I would like to thank the Almighty for His blessings, guidance, and strength, which have inspired me throughout this journey.

I express my heartfelt gratitude to my parents, my in-laws, my wife, my sisters, and my daughter for their unwavering encouragement, patience, and belief in my endeavours. Their constant support has been the foundation of my success.

I also extend my sincere thanks to my director, mentors, colleagues, and peers who have guided me with their valuable insights and constructive feedback.

Lastly, I owe a debt of gratitude to my students and readers, whose curiosity and enthusiasm have continually motivated me to explore, learn, and contribute to the academic and professional community. This book is dedicated to the pursuit of knowledge and the spirit of lifelong learning.

Thank you all for being a part of this meaningful journey.

Dr. Arpan Shrivastava
Author

GENERAL MANAGEMENT

CHAPTER I

Transforming Organizational Culture at DeltaCorp

- **Case Study:**

DeltaCorp, a mid-sized manufacturing company, was struggling with low employee morale, high turnover rates, and declining productivity. The company operated with a rigid hierarchy and minimal employee involvement in decision-making, leading to disengagement and dissatisfaction among its workforce. The CEO, Ms. Anjali Sharma, recognized the need for a cultural transformation to align the organization with modern management practices and retain its competitive edge.

To initiate the change, Ms. Sharma hired a consulting firm specializing in organizational development. The consultants conducted an extensive employee survey, which revealed key issues: lack of recognition, limited opportunities for growth, and poor communication between management and employees. Based on the findings, DeltaCorp implemented several initiatives:

1. **Empowerment through Participation:** The company introduced a participatory decision-making process, encouraging employees at all levels to contribute ideas and solutions. Regular brainstorming sessions and team meetings were held to foster collaboration.
2. **Recognition Programs:** A monthly "Employee Excellence" program was launched to reward outstanding contributions. Employees appreciated the tangible rewards, including gift vouchers, certificates, and public acknowledgement.
3. **Learning and Development:** DeltaCorp invested in training programs to upskill its workforce. A mentorship program paired senior employees with juniors to facilitate knowledge sharing and career development.
4. **Enhanced Communication:** Open forums and quarterly town hall meetings were introduced, where employees could directly address concerns with senior management. A digital platform was also created

for sharing updates and achievements across departments.

Over the next two years, DeltaCorp experienced a remarkable turnaround. Employee satisfaction scores improved by 45%, turnover rates dropped by 30%, and productivity increased by 25%. The participatory approach not only boosted morale but also led to innovative solutions that reduced operational costs by 15%.

Despite the success, challenges remained. Not all employees embraced the changes, and some managers struggled to adapt to the new leadership style. DeltaCorp continues to refine its cultural transformation journey, learning from both successes and setbacks.

- **Questions:**

1. What were the primary issues affecting employee morale and productivity at DeltaCorp?
2. How did participatory decision-making contribute to the company's turnaround?
3. Discuss the role of recognition and reward programs in boosting employee engagement.
4. What challenges might arise when implementing a cultural transformation in an organization?
5. How can DeltaCorp address resistance to change among certain employees and managers?

• • •

CHAPTER II

Supply Chain Optimization at FastMart Retailers

- **Case Study:**

FastMart Retailers, a regional grocery chain, faced frequent stockouts of popular products and excessive inventory of slow-moving items. These inefficiencies not only resulted in lost sales but also increased warehousing costs. Customer complaints about unavailable products and delayed restocking were rising, threatening the company's reputation.

To address these issues, the COO, Mr. Ramesh Kulkarni, initiated a supply chain optimization project. The company collaborated with a supply chain consulting firm to analyze its processes. Key findings included outdated inventory management systems, a lack of real-time data sharing, and poor demand forecasting.

FastMart implemented the following changes:

1. **Technology Integration:** The company invested in a modern inventory management system that provided real-time data on stock levels, sales patterns, and supplier performance.
2. **Demand Forecasting:** Advanced analytics tools were introduced to predict customer demand based on historical data, seasonal trends, and market conditions. This helped the company place more accurate orders with suppliers.
3. **Supplier Collaboration:** FastMart established closer partnerships with key suppliers, enabling just-in-time deliveries and reducing lead times. A vendor scorecard system was implemented to monitor supplier performance.
4. **Employee Training:** Warehouse and store employees received training on using the new technology and understanding demand forecasting techniques.

Within a year, FastMart's stockouts were reduced by 40%, and excess inventory was cut by 25%. Customer satisfaction scores improved significantly, and operational costs decreased, boosting the company's profitability.

However, the company faced initial resistance from employees unfamiliar with the new systems and processes. Additionally, some suppliers struggled to meet the new performance standards, requiring further adjustments to the strategy.

- **Questions:**

1. What were the key inefficiencies in FastMart's supply chain before the optimization?
2. How did technology integration and demand forecasting improve inventory management?
3. Discuss the importance of supplier collaboration in supply chain optimization.
4. What challenges did FastMart face during the implementation of the new systems?
5. How can the company ensure continuous improvement in its supply chain processes?

• • •

CHAPTER III

Crisis Management at AlphaTech Solutions

- **Case Study:**

AlphaTech Solutions, a software development firm, was hit by a cyberattack that compromised sensitive client data and disrupted operations. The attack resulted in reputational damage and potential financial losses due to breached contracts. Clients were demanding answers, and employees were unsure about the company's future.

The CEO, Mr Rahul Deshmukh, took immediate action by assembling a crisis management team comprising IT, legal, and PR professionals. The team implemented the following steps:

1. **Immediate Response:** The IT department isolated affected systems to prevent further damage. Cybersecurity experts were hired to investigate the breach and restore operations.
2. **Transparent Communication:** Clients were informed about the breach within 24 hours, along with assurances of ongoing efforts to address the situation. Regular updates were provided to maintain trust.
3. **Strengthening Security:** The company upgraded its cybersecurity infrastructure, including firewalls, encryption protocols, and multi-factor authentication. Employees were trained on cybersecurity best practices to prevent future breaches.
4. **Reputation Management:** A public relations campaign highlighted the company's swift response and commitment to resolving the issue. Client testimonials and case studies showcasing successful projects were shared to rebuild trust.

Despite initial setbacks, AlphaTech regained client confidence and secured new contracts within six months. The company's proactive approach to crisis management became a benchmark in the industry.

- **Questions:**

1. What were the immediate actions taken by AlphaTech to address the cyberattack?
2. How did transparent communication help in retaining client trust?
3. Discuss the importance of strengthening cybersecurity in today's business environment.
4. What role did reputation management play in AlphaTech's recovery?
5. How can AlphaTech prevent similar crises in the future?

• • •

CHAPTER IV

Sustainable Growth at EcoHome Furnishings

- **Case Study:**

EcoHome Furnishings, a mid-sized furniture manufacturer, was known for its eco-friendly products made from sustainable materials. Despite a loyal customer base, the company struggled with stagnant sales and rising costs. Competitors were launching innovative products, and EcoHome's growth seemed to plateau.

The CEO, Ms. Kavita Mehra, realized the need to rethink the company's strategy to achieve sustainable growth. After extensive brainstorming and consulting with experts, the following initiatives were undertaken:

1. **Product Innovation:** EcoHome invested in research and development to create modular furniture that was affordable, durable, and easy to assemble. This appealed to urban customers who prioritized functionality and style.
2. **Expansion into E-Commerce:** The company launched its e-commerce platform, enabling direct-to-consumer sales. Partnerships with popular online marketplaces increased visibility and sales.
3. **Sustainable Supply Chain:** To address rising costs, EcoHome optimized its supply chain by partnering with local suppliers and adopting energy-efficient production methods. This reduced transportation costs and enhanced its sustainability credentials.
4. **Customer Engagement:** The company introduced a loyalty program and hosted workshops on eco-friendly living. Customers appreciated these efforts, leading to increased brand loyalty.

Within two years, EcoHome's revenue grew by 30%, and operational costs were reduced by 20%. The company's innovative approach attracted media attention, further boosting its brand image. However, the rapid expansion also posed challenges, such as managing increased demand and ensuring consistent quality.

- **Questions:**

1. What challenges did EcoHome face before implementing its new strategy?
2. How did product innovation contribute to the company's growth?
3. Discuss the role of e-commerce in EcoHome's success.
4. What were the benefits of optimizing the supply chain for EcoHome?
5. How can EcoHome address the challenges of rapid expansion?

• • •

CHAPTER V

Leadership Transition at Zenith Pharmaceuticals

- **Case Study:**

Zenith Pharmaceuticals, a family-owned business, faced a major transition when its long-serving CEO and founder, Mr. Arjun Nair, decided to retire. His daughter, Ms. Riya Nair, was named the new CEO. While Riya had a strong educational background and experience in the pharmaceutical industry, employees were sceptical about her leadership capabilities.

To ensure a smooth transition, Riya introduced several initiatives:

1. **Stakeholder Engagement:** Riya held town hall meetings to address employee concerns, outline her vision, and emphasize her commitment to maintaining the company's values.
2. **Leadership Team Restructuring:** She promoted talented employees to key positions, ensuring a mix of experienced leaders and fresh perspectives in decision-making.
3. **Focus on Innovation:** Riya prioritized research and development, launching a new division dedicated to developing affordable generic drugs for underserved markets.
4. **Cultural Transformation:** To foster collaboration and transparency, Riya introduced an open-door policy and encouraged cross-functional teamwork.

While the transition period was challenging, Riya's efforts gradually gained the trust of employees and stakeholders. Within three years, Zenith Pharmaceuticals expanded its market share by 25%, and employee satisfaction scores improved significantly. The company also launched two successful products under Riya's leadership.

- **Questions:**

1. What were the challenges faced during the leadership transition at Zenith Pharmaceuticals?

2. How did Riya address employee skepticism about her leadership?
3. Discuss the importance of innovation in Riya's strategy for Zenith Pharmaceuticals.
4. What role did cultural transformation play in the company's success?
5. How can family-owned businesses prepare for leadership transitions?

• • •

CHAPTER VI

Ethical Dilemma at GlobalText Solutions

- **Case Study:**

GlobalText Solutions, a content outsourcing company, landed a lucrative contract with a global client. However, midway through the project, employees discovered that the client's materials included plagiarized content and potentially offensive material. The project manager, Mr. Rohit Singh, faced an ethical dilemma: continuing the project would boost the company's revenue but compromise its ethical standards.

After discussing the issue with the senior management team, the company decided to:

1. **Pause the Project:** Work on the client's project was temporarily halted to assess the extent of the issue.
2. **Client Communication:** The client was informed about the concerns. GlobalText offered to revise the materials but emphasized the need for original and appropriate content.
3. **Internal Policy Strengthening:** The company implemented stricter guidelines for client onboarding and content quality checks to prevent similar situations in the future.

While the decision led to the loss of the contract, GlobalText's employees and existing clients appreciated the company's commitment to ethical practices. The incident enhanced the company's reputation as a trustworthy service provider.

- **Questions:**

1. What was the ethical dilemma faced by GlobalText Solutions?
2. How did the company balance ethical considerations with business objectives?
3. Discuss the role of transparency in client communication during ethical conflicts.

4. How can companies prevent similar ethical dilemmas in the future?
5. What are the long-term benefits of maintaining ethical standards in business?

• • •

Digital Transformation at FreshMart Supermarkets

- **Case Study:**

FreshMart Supermarkets, a regional grocery chain, faced increasing competition from online retailers. Customers preferred the convenience of online shopping, and FreshMart's foot traffic and sales were declining. To address these challenges, the management decided to embrace digital transformation.

The following initiatives were implemented:

1. **Online Platform Launch:** FreshMart launched an e-commerce website and mobile app, allowing customers to order groceries online with doorstep delivery.
2. **Personalized Marketing:** The company used customer data to send personalized offers and recommendations via email and push notifications.
3. **In-Store Technology:** Self-checkout kiosks and digital price tags were introduced to enhance the in-store shopping experience.
4. **Loyalty Program Integration:** FreshMart's existing loyalty program was integrated into the online platform, enabling customers to earn and redeem points seamlessly across channels.

The digital transformation resulted in a 40% increase in overall sales within 18 months. While online orders grew significantly, in-store foot traffic also stabilized as customers appreciated the enhanced shopping experience. However, FreshMart faced challenges in managing logistics and ensuring timely deliveries, especially during peak seasons.

- **Questions:**

1. What challenges prompted FreshMart to undergo digital transformation?

2. How did the online platform contribute to FreshMart's success?
3. Discuss the role of personalized marketing in improving customer engagement.
4. What operational challenges might arise from digital transformation?
5. How can FreshMart ensure the long-term success of its digital initiatives?

• • •

CHAPTER VIII

Ethical Dilemma at GlobalText Solutions

- **Case Study:**

GlobalText Solutions, a content outsourcing company, landed a lucrative contract with a global client. However, midway through the project, employees discovered that the client's materials included plagiarized content and potentially offensive material. The project manager, Mr. Rohit Singh, faced an ethical dilemma: continuing the project would boost the company's revenue but compromise its ethical standards.

After discussing the issue with the senior management team, the company decided to:

1. **Pause the Project:** Work on the client's project was temporarily halted to assess the extent of the issue.
2. **Client Communication:** The client was informed about the concerns. GlobalText offered to revise the materials but emphasized the need for original and appropriate content.
3. **Internal Policy Strengthening:** The company implemented stricter guidelines for client onboarding and content quality checks to prevent similar situations in the future.

While the decision led to the loss of the contract, GlobalText's employees and existing clients appreciated the company's commitment to ethical practices. The incident enhanced the company's reputation as a trustworthy service provider.

- **Questions:**

1. What was the ethical dilemma faced by GlobalText Solutions?
2. How did the company balance ethical considerations with business objectives?
3. Discuss the role of transparency in client communication during ethical conflicts.

4. How can companies prevent similar ethical dilemmas in the future?
5. What are the long-term benefits of maintaining ethical standards in business?

• • •

Digital Transformation at FreshMart Supermarkets

- **Case Study:**

FreshMart Supermarkets, a regional grocery chain, faced increasing competition from online retailers. Customers preferred the convenience of online shopping, and FreshMart's foot traffic and sales were declining. To address these challenges, the management decided to embrace digital transformation.

The following initiatives were implemented:

1. **Online Platform Launch:** FreshMart launched an e-commerce website and mobile app, allowing customers to order groceries online with doorstep delivery.
2. **Personalized Marketing:** The company used customer data to send personalized offers and recommendations via email and push notifications.
3. **In-Store Technology:** Self-checkout kiosks and digital price tags were introduced to enhance the in-store shopping experience.
4. **Loyalty Program Integration:** FreshMart's existing loyalty program was integrated into the online platform, enabling customers to earn and redeem points seamlessly across channels.

The digital transformation resulted in a 40% increase in overall sales within 18 months. While online orders grew significantly, in-store foot traffic also stabilized as customers appreciated the enhanced shopping experience. However, FreshMart faced challenges in managing logistics and ensuring timely deliveries, especially during peak seasons.

- **Questions:**

1. What challenges prompted FreshMart to undergo digital transformation?

2. How did the online platform contribute to FreshMart's success?
3. Discuss the role of personalized marketing in improving customer engagement.
4. What operational challenges might arise from digital transformation?
5. How can FreshMart ensure the long-term success of its digital initiatives?

• • •

CHAPTER X

Team Conflict Resolution at StarTech Innovations

- **Case Study:**

StarTech Innovations, a technology startup, experienced a major conflict between its product development and marketing teams. The marketing team blamed product delays for missed campaign deadlines, while the product team felt pressured to compromise quality for speed. The conflict disrupted projects and created a toxic work environment.

The CEO, Mr. Sameer Verma, decided to address the issue by:

1. **Facilitating Open Dialogue:** A series of mediated meetings were held to allow both teams to express their concerns and perspectives. The focus was on finding common ground and understanding each team's challenges.
2. **Clarifying Roles and Responsibilities:** Clear guidelines were established to define each team's roles in the project lifecycle, minimizing overlaps and misunderstandings.
3. **Improving Project Management:** A centralized project management tool was introduced to track progress, set realistic deadlines, and ensure transparency.
4. **Building Team Cohesion:** Team-building activities were organized to foster collaboration and mutual respect. Both teams participated in workshops on effective communication and conflict resolution.

Within six months, the conflict was resolved, and productivity improved by 25%. Projects were completed on time, and employee satisfaction scores increased. The experience also strengthened StarTech's commitment to proactive conflict management.

- **Questions:**

1. What were the main causes of conflict between the teams at StarTech Innovations?
2. How did open dialogue contribute to resolving the conflict?
3. Discuss the importance of clarifying roles and responsibilities in teamwork.
4. What role do team-building activities play in conflict resolution?
5. How can StarTech prevent similar conflicts in the future?

• • •

CHAPTER XI

Strategic Downsizing at Apex Technologies

- **Case Study:**

Apex Technologies, a global IT firm, experienced a sudden decline in revenue due to changing market trends and intense competition. The company's legacy products were losing relevance, and its attempts to penetrate emerging markets had not yielded the expected results. To stabilize operations and reduce costs, the management decided to undertake strategic downsizing.

The process began with a detailed analysis of underperforming business units. After identifying areas for optimization, the company implemented the following measures:

1. **Workforce Restructuring:** Apex reduced its workforce by 15%, focusing on roles that were redundant or could be automated. The layoffs were accompanied by severance packages and career transition support.
2. **Product Portfolio Optimization:** The company phased out outdated products and invested in developing innovative solutions aligned with market needs.
3. **Operational Efficiency:** Apex streamlined its processes, adopting cloud-based systems to reduce overhead costs.
4. **Employee Communication:** Management ensured transparent communication throughout the downsizing process, addressing employee concerns and maintaining morale.

While the downsizing improved Apex's financial performance, it also created challenges such as increased workload for remaining employees and potential damage to the company's reputation. Over time, Apex regained profitability and launched successful new products, but employee retention remained a concern.

- **Questions:**

1. What factors led to Apex Technologies' decision to downsize?
2. How did product portfolio optimization contribute to the company's recovery?
3. Discuss the importance of transparent communication during downsizing.
4. What challenges might arise after workforce restructuring?
5. How can Apex address employee retention in the long term?

• • •

CHAPTER XII

Crisis Management at GreenLife Organics

- **Case Study:**

GreenLife Organics, a popular organic food brand, faced a major crisis when reports surfaced about pesticide residues in one of its flagship products. Customers took to social media to express their anger, and retailers began pulling the product from their shelves.

Sales plummeted, and the company's reputation was at stake.

The management acted swiftly to address the crisis:

1. **Product Recall:** GreenLife immediately recalled the affected product from all retail outlets, prioritizing customer safety over financial losses.
2. **Transparency and Communication:** The company issued public statements acknowledging the issue, apologizing to customers, and outlining steps to resolve the problem.
3. **Investigation and Quality Control:** An independent investigation was launched to identify the source of contamination. GreenLife also enhanced its quality control processes to prevent future incidents.
4. **Customer Assurance:** The company offered refunds and discounts to affected customers and launched a campaign to rebuild trust.

Within six months, GreenLife regained customer confidence and restored its market share. The incident served as a wake-up call, prompting the company to adopt stricter quality standards.

However, the crisis highlighted the need for better supply chain management and proactive risk assessment.

- **Questions:**

1. What steps did GreenLife take to manage the crisis?
2. How did transparency help GreenLife rebuild customer trust?
3. Discuss the role of quality control in preventing such incidents.
4. What lessons can GreenLife learn from this crisis?

5. How can companies prepare for potential crises in the future?

• • •

26

CHAPTER XIII

Diversity and Inclusion at Unity Bank

- **Case Study:**

Unity Bank, a leading financial institution, launched a diversity and inclusion (D&I) initiative to create a more equitable workplace. The initiative aimed to address gender disparities, promote cultural sensitivity, and provide opportunities for underrepresented groups.

Key measures included:

1. **Diversity Hiring:** Unity Bank set specific goals for hiring women and minorities in leadership roles. Partnerships with organizations promoting workplace diversity helped the bank identify suitable candidates.
2. **Employee Training:** Workshops on unconscious bias, cultural competence, and inclusive leadership were conducted across all levels of the organization.
3. **Employee Resource Groups (ERGs):** ERGs for women, LGBTQ+ employees, and minority groups were established to provide support and foster a sense of belonging.
4. **Policy Changes:** The bank introduced flexible work arrangements, parental leave policies, and mentorship programs to support employees from diverse backgrounds.

The D&I initiative led to a 30% increase in female leadership within three years and improved employee satisfaction scores. Unity Bank's inclusive culture attracted top talent and enhanced its reputation as an employer of choice. However, challenges such as resistance to change and unconscious bias persisted, requiring ongoing efforts.

- **Questions:**

1. What steps did Unity Bank take to promote diversity and inclusion?
2. How can employee training contribute to a more inclusive workplace?

3. Discuss the role of ERGs in fostering diversity.
4. What challenges might arise in implementing D&I initiatives?
5. How can Unity Bank ensure the long-term success of its D&I strategy?

• • •

CHAPTER XIV

Expansion Challenges at Bistro Delights

- **Case Study:**

Bistro Delights, a popular chain of casual dining restaurants, decided to expand into international markets after achieving success in its home country. The management chose Southeast Asia as the initial target, considering the region's growing middle class and demand for global cuisines.

However, the expansion presented several challenges:

1. **Cultural Differences:** Bistro Delights faced difficulties adapting its menu to local tastes. Popular dishes in its home country did not resonate with customers in Southeast Asia.
2. **Regulatory Compliance:** Navigating complex regulations in different countries delayed the opening of new outlets.
3. **Supply Chain Issues:** Sourcing fresh ingredients locally while maintaining consistency in quality proved challenging.
4. **Brand Awareness:** Bistro Delights was relatively unknown in the new markets, requiring significant investment in marketing and promotions.

To address these challenges, the company partnered with local consultants to understand customer preferences, adapted its menu to include regional flavors, and invested in training programs for staff. Despite initial setbacks, Bistro Delights gradually established itself in Southeast Asia, achieving profitability within three years.

- **Questions:**

1. What challenges did Bistro Delights face during its international expansion?
2. How did cultural differences impact the company's operations?
3. Discuss the importance of local partnerships in overcoming expansion challenges.

4. What role does marketing play in building brand awareness in new markets?

5. How can Bistro Delights sustain its success in international markets?

• • •

CHAPTER XV

Innovation in Employee Engagement at SmartWorks Inc.

- **Case Study:**

SmartWorks Inc., a mid-sized IT services company, struggled with low employee engagement and high turnover rates. Recognizing the need to address this issue, the management launched an employee engagement program called "Empower."

The program focused on the following initiatives:

1. **Flexible Work Options:** Employees were given the choice to work remotely or adopt flexible schedules, improving work-life balance.
2. **Skill Development:** SmartWorks introduced online training programs and certifications to help employees enhance their skills and advance their careers.
3. **Recognition and Rewards:** A points-based rewards system was implemented to recognize employees for their contributions. Points could be redeemed for gifts or additional paid leave.
4. **Employee Feedback:** Regular surveys and town hall meetings were conducted to gather employee feedback and address concerns.
5. **Wellness Programs:** The company organized wellness initiatives such as fitness challenges, mental health workshops, and free counseling services.

The "Empower" program resulted in a 25% reduction in turnover rates and a significant improvement in employee satisfaction scores. SmartWorks became known for its employee-friendly culture, which also attracted top talent. However, sustaining the program required continuous investment and adaptability to changing employee needs.

- **Questions:**

1. What were the key components of the "Empower" program at SmartWorks Inc.?
2. How did flexible work options contribute to improved employee engagement?
3. Discuss the role of recognition and rewards in retaining employees.
4. What challenges might SmartWorks face in sustaining its employee engagement program?
5. How can companies measure the success of employee engagement initiatives?

• • •

CHAPTER XVI

Effective Communication in Teams

- **Case Study:**

Lisa was recently promoted to lead a team of six employees at a mid-sized marketing firm. While Lisa had strong technical skills, she struggled with clear communication. During meetings, she often assumed her team understood her instructions without elaborating. This led to confusion among team members, missed deadlines, and duplicated efforts. Frustrated, Lisa blamed the team for their lack of initiative.

Recognizing the problem, Lisa's manager suggested she adopt a more structured communication style. Lisa began using clear agendas for meetings, summarizing key points, and encouraging team members to ask questions. She also implemented weekly check-ins to monitor progress and clarify expectations. Over time, her team's performance improved significantly, and projects were completed more efficiently.

- **Questions:**

1. What were the primary communication issues faced by Lisa?
2. How did these issues impact her team's performance?
3. What steps did Lisa take to improve her communication? Were they effective?
4. How can managers ensure clarity in team communication?
5. If you were in Lisa's position, what additional steps might you take?

• • •

CHAPTER XVII

Managing Conflict in the Workplace

- **Case Study:**

At BrightTech Solutions, tensions arose between two key employees, Sarah and Mark, who were working on a high-profile project. Sarah felt Mark was overly critical and dismissive of her ideas during team discussions. Mark, on the other hand, believed Sarah's contributions lacked depth and focus. Their disagreements created a toxic environment that affected the entire team.

The project manager, David, decided to address the issue directly. He scheduled a mediation meeting where both Sarah and Mark were encouraged to share their perspectives openly. David emphasized the importance of mutual respect and collaboration. He also proposed a clear division of responsibilities to minimize overlaps and potential conflicts.

Following the meeting, Sarah and Mark worked on building mutual trust by acknowledging each other's strengths. With improved communication and a defined structure, the team successfully completed the project on time.

- **Questions:**

1. What were the main sources of conflict between Sarah and Mark?
2. How did their conflict impact the team's dynamics and productivity?
3. What role did David play in resolving the conflict? Was his approach effective?
4. How can workplace conflicts be managed proactively?
5. Suggest additional strategies to foster collaboration in high-stakes projects.

• • •

CHAPTER XVIII

Delegation Challenges for New Managers

- **Case Study:**

John was recently promoted to a managerial role in a software development firm. Eager to prove himself, he decided to oversee every aspect of his team's work. Instead of delegating tasks, he micromanaged the team, reviewing even minor details. This led to delays, frustration among team members, and an overall decrease in productivity.

After receiving feedback from his team and his own manager, John realized the importance of trust and delegation. He started assigning tasks based on team members' strengths and set clear expectations for deliverables. John also focused on providing support and feedback without interfering unnecessarily. Over time, John's team felt more empowered, and their performance improved significantly.

- **Questions:**

1. Why did John initially struggle with delegation?
2. How did his micromanagement affect the team's morale and productivity?
3. What changes did John implement to improve his management style?
4. How can managers identify tasks suitable for delegation?
5. What are the risks of over-delegating, and how can they be avoided?

• • •

CHAPTER XIX

Adapting to Change in the Workplace

- **Case Study:**

Global Retail Co. decided to implement a new inventory management system to streamline operations. While the leadership team was excited about the change, many employees resisted, citing lack of training and fear of job redundancies. Productivity dipped as employees struggled to adapt.

To address the resistance, the company's HR team organized training sessions to familiarize employees with the new system. Managers also held one-on-one meetings to address concerns and highlight how the system would benefit both employees and the company. Over time, employees became more confident, and the new system led to significant improvements in efficiency and accuracy.

- **Questions:**

1. Why did employees resist the implementation of the new system?
2. What actions did the company take to overcome resistance to change?
3. How did addressing employee concerns improve the outcome of the change process?
4. What lessons can be learned about managing organizational change?
5. Suggest additional strategies for ensuring successful change implementation.

• • •

CHAPTER XX

Ethical Decision-Making in Business

- **Case Study:**

Megan, a product manager at a consumer electronics company, discovered that one of their new products had a minor defect. While the defect wouldn't pose safety risks, it could lead to customer dissatisfaction. Megan's supervisor suggested launching the product as planned to avoid delaying the release and incurring additional costs.

Megan felt conflicted. After consulting with her team and gathering data, she presented a plan to address the defect before launch. Although it required a short delay, the company avoided potential backlash and maintained customer trust.

- **Questions:**

1. What ethical dilemma did Megan face?
2. Why might her supervisor have suggested launching the product despite the defect?
3. What steps did Megan take to address the issue?
4. How can businesses balance ethical considerations with operational pressures?
5. Share an example of an ethical decision-making framework that could guide managers

$$\bullet \ \bullet \ \bullet$$

CHAPTER XXI

Transforming Team Dynamics – Enhancing Productivity and Engagement

Case Study:

Rachel was appointed to lead a team that had been underperforming for several months at a consulting firm. Team members appeared disengaged, often submitting work late and of low quality. After her initial observations, Rachel realized that the team lacked clear goals and recognition for their efforts.

To address the situation, Rachel held a meeting to discuss team challenges and gather input on potential solutions. She established SMART (Specific, Measurable, Achievable, Relevant, Time-bound) goals for the team and created a rewards program to acknowledge outstanding performance. Rachel also organized team-building activities to improve morale and foster collaboration.

Within three months, the team's productivity increased, and they started meeting deadlines consistently. Employees felt more valued and motivated, contributing innovative ideas to projects.

Questions:

1. What were the primary reasons for the team's underperformance?
2. How did Rachel address the challenges within the team?
3. Why are clear goals important for team performance?
4. How can recognition programs influence employee motivation?
5. What additional strategies could Rachel implement to sustain team engagement?

● ● ●

CHAPTER XXII

Balancing Innovation with Risk Management

- **Case Study:**

A tech startup, InnovateNow, prided itself on its culture of innovation. However, this culture sometimes led to excessive risk-taking. The company launched several projects without proper market research, resulting in significant financial losses.

To address this, the CEO introduced a new process requiring project proposals to undergo a thorough risk assessment before approval. InnovateNow also established a committee to evaluate potential risks and benefits of proposed projects. Employees were encouraged to innovate within a structured framework that balanced creativity with practicality.

As a result, InnovateNow's success rate for new projects improved, and the company achieved sustainable growth.

- **Questions:**

1. What were the consequences of excessive risk-taking at InnovateNow?
2. How did the introduction of structured processes benefit the company?
3. Why is it important to balance innovation with risk management?
4. How can companies encourage innovation without compromising financial stability?
5. Suggest tools or frameworks for effective risk assessment in business.

• • •

CHAPTER XXIII

Addressing High Employee Turnover

- **Case Study:**

An e-commerce company, ShopEase, faced a growing challenge of high employee turnover, particularly in its customer service department. Exit interviews revealed that employees were leaving due to limited growth opportunities, low morale, and a lack of recognition for their efforts. The constant turnover disrupted operations and increased hiring costs.

To tackle the issue, the HR team launched a career development program, offering employees access to training and mentorship. The company also introduced a monthly recognition program to reward outstanding contributions. Managers were trained to provide regular feedback and foster an inclusive work environment.

Over the next year, employee turnover dropped significantly, and morale improved. Employees reported feeling more engaged and motivated to grow within the organization.

- **Questions:**

1. What were the primary factors contributing to high employee turnover at ShopEase?
2. How did the HR team address these challenges?
3. Why is employee recognition important in retaining staff?
4. What role do growth opportunities play in employee retention?
5. Suggest additional initiatives that could further reduce turnover.

• • •

CHAPTER XXIV

Transformational Leadership in Action

- **Scenario:**

A medium-sized IT company, TechNova, was facing declining employee morale and increasing turnover rates. The CEO, Rachel Adams, decided to bring in a new manager, David Lee, to revitalize the company's operations and culture. David was known for his transformational leadership style. Within the first three months, he held one-on-one meetings with employees, identified key pain points, and implemented initiatives to improve communication and collaboration. He also introduced flexible work policies, professional development programs, and regular team-building activities.

As a result, employee satisfaction scores increased by 40%, and turnover rates dropped significantly. The company's quarterly revenues grew by 15% as teams became more cohesive and efficient. However, some senior managers resisted the changes, arguing that David's methods were too unconventional.

- **Questions:**

1. What are the key elements of transformational leadership demonstrated by David?
2. How did David address the issues of employee morale and turnover?
3. What challenges might David face in dealing with resistance from senior managers?
4. Suggest ways to overcome resistance to change in organizations.
5. How can the success of transformational leadership initiatives be measured?

• • •

CHAPTER XXV

Decision–Making Under Uncertainty

- **Scenario:**

GreenTech, a renewable energy startup, faced a dilemma when a key investor pulled out at the last minute. The company had to decide whether to delay the launch of its new solar product or proceed with limited funds. The leadership team, led by CEO Maria Chen, conducted a risk analysis.

They identified potential cost-cutting measures and alternative funding sources, such as government grants and crowdfunding. After deliberation, they decided to launch on schedule with a leaner budget and secured additional funds through a successful crowdfunding campaign.

Questions:

1. What decision-making approaches did GreenTech use to address the funding crisis?
2. How can risk analysis help in making strategic decisions?
3. What are the pros and cons of proceeding with limited resources?
4. Suggest alternative strategies GreenTech could have used to handle the situation.
5. How can startups build resilience against financial uncertainties?

• • •

CHAPTER XXVI

Managing Diversity in the Workplace

- **Scenario:**

GlobalFoods, a multinational company, faced challenges in managing its diverse workforce. Employees from different cultural backgrounds had difficulties collaborating due to language barriers and differing work styles. To address this, the HR team implemented a comprehensive diversity training program and introduced cross-cultural mentoring initiatives.

They also established an internal communication platform where employees could share their ideas and experiences. Over six months, workplace conflicts decreased by 25%, and employee engagement levels improved.

- **Questions:**

1. What steps did GlobalFoods take to address diversity challenges?
2. How can cross-cultural mentoring benefit an organization?
3. What role does effective communication play in managing diversity?
4. How can companies measure the success of diversity initiatives?
5. What additional strategies can GlobalFoods implement to promote inclusion?

• • •

Crisis Management During a Product Recall

- **Scenario:**

An electronics company, SparkTech, discovered a safety issue in one of its bestselling smartphones. The company decided to recall the product immediately, even though it meant incurring significant financial losses. CEO Alan Carter held a press conference to apologize to customers and outline the steps being taken to resolve the issue.

The company offered refunds and free replacements, along with an extended warranty for the affected models. Although the recall initially hurt SparkTech's reputation, its transparency and customer-focused approach eventually won back consumer trust.

Questions:

1. What were the key elements of SparkTech's crisis management strategy?
2. How did transparency help SparkTech regain customer trust?
3. What are the potential risks of delaying a product recall?
4. Suggest ways to prevent similar issues in the future.
5. How can companies balance financial losses with ethical responsibility?

• • •

CHAPTER XXVIII

Strategic Planning for Market Expansion

Scenario:

FashionForward, a boutique clothing brand, planned to expand into international markets. The leadership team conducted a SWOT analysis and identified Southeast Asia as a promising region due to its growing middle class and demand for premium fashion.

They adapted their marketing strategy to suit local tastes and partnered with regional influencers to build brand awareness. Within a year, sales in the new market exceeded expectations, contributing to a 20% overall revenue growth.

Questions:

1. How did the SWOT analysis help FashionForward identify new opportunities?
2. What factors should companies consider when entering international markets?
3. How can partnerships with local influencers benefit market expansion?
4. What challenges might arise in adapting to new markets?
5. Suggest additional strategies to ensure the success of international expansion.

• • •

CHAPTER XXIX

The Impact of Ethical Leadership

- **Scenario:**

Ecometrix, a logistics company, faced allegations of unethical practices by a supplier. CEO Jack Wilson immediately launched an internal investigation and terminated the contract with the supplier. He introduced stricter supplier vetting processes and held workshops to reinforce the company's ethical standards. Jack's actions reassured stakeholders, and the company's reputation for integrity remained intact. This approach also attracted new clients who valued ethical practices.

- **Questions:**

1. What actions did Jack take to address the allegations?
2. How does ethical leadership benefit an organization?
3. What challenges can arise when enforcing ethical standards?
4. Suggest ways to build a culture of integrity within an organization.
5. How can companies effectively communicate their ethical policies to stakeholders?

• • •

CHAPTER XXX

Implementing Agile Methodologies

- **Scenario:**

InnovSoft, a software development firm, struggled with missed deadlines and low client satisfaction. The leadership team decided to adopt agile methodologies, including daily stand-ups, sprints, and retrospectives.

They trained employees on agile practices and empowered teams to make decisions collaboratively. Over time, project timelines became more predictable, and client satisfaction scores increased by 30%.

- **Questions:**

1. What challenges did InnovSoft face before implementing agile methodologies?
2. How did agile practices improve team performance?
3. What are the benefits of empowering teams in a workplace?
4. Suggest additional ways to enhance agile implementation.
5. How can the impact of agile methodologies be measured?

• • •

CHAPTER XXXI

Innovation Through Collaboration

- **Scenario:**

BrightIdeas, a consumer electronics company, launched an internal innovation challenge to encourage employees to propose new product ideas. The winning idea, a portable solar charger, was developed into a marketable product.

BrightIdeas provided resources and support to the team behind the idea, resulting in a successful product launch that captured a significant market share in the sustainable technology segment.

- **Questions:**

1. How did the innovation challenge foster creativity at BrightIdeas?
2. What role does collaboration play in driving innovation?
3. How can companies support employees in turning ideas into reality?
4. What are the potential risks of innovation initiatives?
5. Suggest additional strategies to promote a culture of innovation.

• • •

CHAPTER XXXII

Conflict Resolution in Teams

- **Scenario:**

At MedEquip, a healthcare equipment manufacturer, a conflict arose between the sales and marketing teams over resource allocation. The conflict began affecting overall productivity. The company's HR manager facilitated a series of mediation sessions, allowing both teams to voice their concerns and find common ground. They agreed on a shared resource allocation plan, which improved interdepartmental collaboration and restored productivity.

- **Questions:**

1. What steps did the HR manager take to resolve the conflict?
2. How can effective conflict resolution improve team dynamics?
3. What are the risks of unresolved conflicts in the workplace?
4. Suggest additional strategies to prevent interdepartmental conflicts.
5. How can organizations foster a culture of collaboration?

• • •

CHAPTER XXXIII

Leveraging Technology for Operational Efficiency

- **Scenario:**

FreshHarvest, an organic farming company, struggled with inefficiencies in its supply chain. The company implemented a new inventory management system powered by AI to track and optimize stock levels. This technology reduced waste by 25% and improved order fulfillment rates by 30%.

FreshHarvest's operational costs also decreased, allowing the company to invest in expanding its product line.

- **Questions:**

1. How did FreshHarvest use technology to address its challenges?
2. What are the benefits of AI in supply chain management?
3. How can companies measure the ROI of new technologies?
4. Suggest additional ways to improve operational efficiency using technology.
5. What challenges might arise during the implementation of new systems?

• • •

MARKETING

CHAPTER XXXIV

The Rise of Influencer Marketing

- **Case Study:**

In the digital age, influencer marketing has emerged as one of the most powerful tools for brands to connect with their target audience. Companies partner with influencers—individuals with a significant social media following—to promote their products or services. One notable example is a fitness brand that collaborated with a popular health influencer to launch a new line of protein supplements.

The influencer created engaging content, including workout routines and recipes using the supplements, which resonated with their audience.

The campaign resulted in a 35% increase in sales within the first three months. Moreover, the brand's social media following grew by 50%, indicating enhanced engagement and awareness.However, influencer marketing also comes with challenges. Brands must carefully select influencers whose values align with their own.

A mismatch can lead to credibility issues and backlash from consumers. Influencer marketing continues to evolve, with micro-influencers gaining prominence. These influencers have smaller but highly engaged audiences, making them an effective option for niche markets.

The fitness brand's success highlights the potential of this marketing strategy when executed thoughtfully.

- **Questions:**

1. What factors contributed to the success of the fitness brand's influencer marketing campaign?
2. What are the potential risks of working with influencers, and how can brands mitigate them?
3. How does the engagement level of micro-influencers compare to that of macro-influencers?
4. In your opinion, what industries can benefit most from influencer marketing, and why?

CHAPTER XXXV

Rebranding a Legacy Brand

- **Case Study:**

A well-established beverage company faced declining sales as younger consumers gravitated toward healthier options. To stay relevant, the company decided to rebrand. They introduced a new product line of organic, low-calorie drinks and revamped their packaging to appeal to a modern audience. Additionally, the company launched a digital campaign focusing on sustainability and health, leveraging social media platforms to engage with millennials and Gen Z consumers.

The rebranding effort paid off. Within a year, the company reported a 20% increase in market share among younger demographics. The new product line became the fastest-growing segment in their portfolio. However, the transition wasn't without challenges. The company faced criticism from loyal customers who felt alienated by the shift in focus.

This case underscores the importance of balancing innovation with brand heritage. It also highlights the need for thorough market research and effective communication to navigate rebranding efforts successfully.

- **Questions:**

1. What strategies did the beverage company use to appeal to younger consumers?
2. How can companies balance the need to innovate with maintaining their existing customer base?
3. What role does social media play in successful rebranding campaigns?
4. Discuss the potential pitfalls of rebranding and how they can be addressed.

• • •

CHAPTER XXXVI

The Power of Data-Driven Marketing

- **Case Study:**

A retail company used advanced analytics to understand customer behavior and preferences. By analyzing purchase history, browsing patterns, and demographic data, the company personalized marketing campaigns for different customer segments. For instance, they sent targeted email promotions featuring products based on individual shopping habits. They also implemented a dynamic pricing strategy, offering discounts on items that customers frequently viewed but hadn't purchased.

The results were impressive. Conversion rates for email campaigns increased by 40%, and customer retention improved by 25%. Additionally, the company's overall revenue grew by 15% in a year. However, data-driven marketing raised concerns about privacy and data security. The company invested in robust security measures and transparent communication to address these issues.

This case illustrates the transformative potential of leveraging data in marketing while emphasizing the need for ethical practices and customer trust.

- **Questions:**

1. How did the retail company use data to enhance its marketing efforts?
2. What are the ethical considerations involved in data-driven marketing?
3. How can companies ensure transparency and build trust when using customer data?
4. What are the advantages and challenges of implementing a dynamic pricing strategy?

• • •

CHAPTER XXXVII

Launching a Viral Campaign

- **Case Study:**

A tech startup aimed to create buzz for its innovative gadget. The company developed a creative marketing campaign centered around a viral video featuring the product's unique features. The video, shared across multiple social media platforms, showcased the gadget's capabilities in an entertaining and relatable way. To amplify the campaign, the company encouraged user-generated content by hosting a contest where customers could share their own creative uses of the product.

The video garnered over 10 million views in the first week, and the contest received thousands of entries. The startup's website traffic increased tenfold, and pre-orders for the gadget exceeded expectations. Despite the success, the company faced logistical challenges in meeting the surge in demand, leading to some customer dissatisfaction.

This case highlights the impact of creativity and audience engagement in achieving viral success while underlining the importance of operational preparedness.

- **Questions:**

1. What elements contributed to the viral success of the tech startup's campaign?
2. How can user-generated content enhance marketing campaigns?
3. What steps can companies take to prepare for increased demand resulting from viral campaigns?
4. Discuss the potential risks of relying on viral marketing as a primary strategy.

• • •

CHAPTER XXXVIII

Social Media Strategy — Coca-Cola's "Share a Coke" Campaign

- **Case Study:**

Coca-Cola's "Share a Coke" campaign, launched in 2011 in Australia, is a shining example of a successful personalized marketing strategy. The idea was simple yet powerful: replace the iconic Coca-Cola logo on bottles with popular names, encouraging customers to "Share a Coke" with friends and loved ones. This campaign quickly expanded to other countries, adapting the names and messages to suit local markets.

The campaign's genius lay in its ability to create a sense of personal connection between the consumer and the product. By personalizing the bottles, Coca-Cola tapped into the universal human desire for recognition and individuality. This sense of connection was further amplified through social media, where consumers were encouraged to share photos of their personalized bottles, using hashtags like #ShareaCoke. The campaign's social media strategy turned customers into brand ambassadors, exponentially increasing its reach.

Coca-Cola also leveraged experiential marketing to make the campaign more interactive. Vending machines were installed in malls and events, allowing customers to print their names on Coca-Cola bottles in real time. This experiential component created memorable moments and deeper engagement.

The results were staggering. Coca-Cola reported a significant increase in sales, with young adults being particularly engaged by the campaign. In some markets, the campaign boosted consumption by over 7%. The brand also saw a surge in social media interactions, with millions of photos and videos shared online.

- **Questions:**

1. Why was personalization crucial to the success of the "Share a Coke" campaign?
2. How did Coca-Cola effectively use social media to enhance the campaign's reach?
3. What role did experiential marketing play in deepening consumer engagement?
4. Could a similar campaign work today, or has the market evolved too much?

• • •

CHAPTER XXXIX

Influencer Marketing — Glossier's Rise to Fame

- **Case Study:**

Glossier, a beauty brand founded in 2014 by Emily Weiss, disrupted the cosmetics industry with its unique approach to marketing. Unlike traditional beauty brands that relied heavily on glossy magazine ads and celebrity endorsements, Glossier turned to micro-influencers and everyday users to create buzz around its products. By prioritizing customer testimonials and user-generated content, the brand built a loyal community that felt personally invested in its success.

Glossier's marketing strategy began with its roots as a blog, "Into The Gloss." Emily Weiss used the platform to connect with readers and discuss real beauty routines. When Glossier launched, it already had a built-in audience of dedicated followers who trusted Weiss's vision. The brand's mantra, "Skin first, makeup second," resonated with millennials and Gen Z consumers who valued authenticity over perfection.

Social media, particularly Instagram, was a cornerstone of Glossier's growth. The brand encouraged customers to share their experiences, tagging @Glossier and using branded hashtags. This created a continuous stream of organic content that felt genuine and relatable. Glossier also collaborated with micro-influencers—individuals with smaller but highly engaged audiences—to further spread its message. This approach proved effective because micro-influencers often have stronger personal connections with their followers, leading to higher trust and credibility.

As a result, Glossier achieved remarkable growth. Within five years, it became a billion-dollar brand, boasting a cult following and a direct-to-consumer model that revolutionized the beauty industry.

- **Questions:**

1. What role did micro-influencers play in Glossier's marketing strategy?
2. How did user-generated content contribute to the brand's success?

3. Why was Glossier's focus on authenticity crucial in appealing to its target audience?
4. What challenges might arise for other brands trying to replicate this strategy?

• • •

CHAPTER XL

Content Marketing — HubSpot's Inbound Marketing Strategy

- **Case Study:**

HubSpot, a leading provider of CRM and marketing software, has become synonymous with the concept of inbound marketing. The company's strategy revolves around creating valuable, educational content to attract and retain customers. By positioning itself as a trusted resource, HubSpot successfully established thought leadership in the marketing and sales space.

HubSpot's content marketing strategy includes a robust mix of blogs, eBooks, webinars, and online courses. The company's blog covers a wide range of topics, from SEO best practices to social media trends, appealing to marketers, sales professionals, and business owners. Additionally, HubSpot's free tools, such as website graders and email marketing templates, provide immediate value to users while introducing them to the company's paid services.

Another key component of HubSpot's strategy is its emphasis on data-driven insights. By tracking user interactions, the company can deliver personalized recommendations and content to its audience, ensuring a more relevant experience. This approach not only builds trust but also nurtures leads through the sales funnel.

The results speak for themselves. HubSpot's focus on inbound marketing helped it grow from a startup to a publicly traded company with a valuation exceeding $10 billion. Its success demonstrates the power of providing value first to earn customer loyalty.

- **Questions:**

1. How did HubSpot's content marketing strategy establish it as a thought leader?

2. Why is providing free tools and resources an effective way to attract customers?

3. What role does personalization play in the success of inbound marketing?

4. How can smaller companies replicate HubSpot's strategy on a limited budget?

• • •

CHAPTER XLI

The Rise of Patanjali

- **Case Study:**

Patanjali Ayurved, founded by Baba Ramdev and Acharya Balkrishna in 2006, revolutionized the Indian FMCG market with its focus on Ayurvedic and natural products. Within a decade, it posed a serious challenge to established players like Hindustan Unilever, Dabur, and ITC. The brand capitalized on the rising demand for natural and chemical-free products and leveraged Baba Ramdev's existing popularity as a yoga guru.

Patanjali's marketing strategy included emphasizing its "Made in India" ethos and promoting its products as affordable and natural alternatives. The company used a mix of traditional and digital media, with Baba Ramdev often featuring prominently in advertisements. Its distribution strategy also played a significant role, with products being available in exclusive Patanjali outlets and major retail stores.

Despite its success, Patanjali faced criticism over quality control issues and over-reliance on Baba Ramdev's personal brand. However, its ability to tap into Indian consumers' preference for Ayurvedic products remains a significant factor in its growth.

- **Questions:**

1. What were the key factors behind Patanjali's success in the Indian FMCG market?
2. How did Patanjali's marketing strategy differentiate it from its competitors?
3. What are the potential risks associated with over-reliance on a single brand ambassador?
4. Suggest strategies for Patanjali to address quality control issues while maintaining its growth.

• • •

CHAPTER XLII

Coca–Cola's "Share a Coke" Campaign

- **Case Study:**

Coca-Cola launched its "Share a Coke" campaign in Australia in 2011. The campaign replaced the iconic Coca-Cola logo on bottles with popular names, encouraging consumers to find and share bottles with the names of their friends and loved ones. This personalized approach created an emotional connection with the brand and led to a significant increase in sales.

The campaign's success in Australia prompted Coca-Cola to roll it out in over 80 countries. The use of social media played a crucial role, as consumers shared pictures of their personalized Coke bottles, further amplifying the campaign's reach.

However, the campaign faced challenges in regions with diverse languages and cultural sensitivities, requiring Coca-Cola to customize its approach. Despite these challenges, "Share a Coke" remains one of the brand's most successful marketing initiatives.

- **Questions:**

1. How did the "Share a Coke" campaign create an emotional connection with consumers?
2. Discuss the role of personalization in Coca-Cola's marketing strategy.
3. What challenges did Coca-Cola face in implementing the campaign globally?
4. Suggest ways Coca-Cola can sustain consumer engagement beyond the campaign.

• • •

CHAPTER XLIII

Zomato's Quirky Social Media Marketing

- **Case Study:**

Zomato, the Indian food delivery and restaurant aggregator, is known for its quirky and relatable social media campaigns. Its content often includes humorous takes on trending topics, memes, and creative wordplay. This strategy has helped Zomato build a strong online presence and engage with its target audience, primarily millennials and Gen Z.

One such campaign was the "Ghar ka Khana, Sabse Achha" ad during the COVID-19 lockdown, which highlighted the importance of home-cooked food while subtly promoting its services. Zomato's use of data-driven insights and creative storytelling has also been key to its success.

However, Zomato's approach has occasionally drawn criticism for being too edgy or controversial. Balancing creativity with brand image and audience sensitivities remains a challenge for the company.

- **Questions:**

1. What makes Zomato's social media strategy effective in engaging its audience?
2. How does Zomato balance humor with brand promotion in its campaigns?
3. Discuss the potential risks of using edgy or controversial content in marketing.
4. Propose strategies for Zomato to expand its audience while maintaining its unique brand voice.

● ● ●

CHAPTER XLIV

Nike's "Just Do It" Campaign

- **Case Study:**

Nike's "Just Do It" campaign, launched in 1988, is one of the most iconic marketing campaigns in history. The slogan resonated with people worldwide, inspiring them to push their limits and achieve their goals. Nike used celebrity endorsements from athletes like Michael Jordan, Serena Williams, and Cristiano Ronaldo to reinforce the message of perseverance and excellence.

The campaign's success lies in its ability to appeal to both professional athletes and everyday individuals. Over the years, Nike has continued to evolve the campaign by incorporating themes of social justice, diversity, and inclusivity, such as the Colin Kaepernick ad in 2018, which sparked global conversations.

Despite its success, the campaign has also faced backlash, with critics accusing Nike of being politically divisive. However, the company's commitment to its values has strengthened its brand loyalty among its core audience.

- **Questions:**

1. How did the "Just Do It" campaign contribute to Nike's brand identity?
2. Discuss the role of celebrity endorsements in Nike's marketing strategy.
3. What are the risks and rewards of incorporating social issues into marketing campaigns?
4. Suggest ways Nike can continue to innovate its "Just Do It" campaign to stay relevant.

· · ·

CHAPTER XLV

Amazon's Customer–Centric Approach

- **Case Study:**

Amazon's rise to dominance in e-commerce is largely attributed to its unwavering focus on customer satisfaction. From its early days as an online bookstore, Amazon expanded into a global marketplace offering everything from electronics to groceries. The company's innovations, such as one-click ordering, same-day delivery, and personalized recommendations, have redefined the shopping experience.

Amazon's marketing strategy revolves around convenience, competitive pricing, and customer reviews. Its Prime membership program, which offers benefits like free shipping and access to streaming services, has further strengthened customer loyalty. The company also invests heavily in data analytics to understand consumer behavior and tailor its offerings.

However, Amazon has faced criticism over labor practices and its impact on small businesses. Addressing these issues while maintaining its growth is a key challenge for the company.

- **Questions:**

1. How does Amazon's focus on customer satisfaction drive its success?
2. Discuss the role of technology in Amazon's marketing and operations.
3. What are the ethical challenges associated with Amazon's business practices?
4. Suggest strategies for Amazon to address criticisms while sustaining its growth.

• • •

CHAPTER XLVI

The Rise of Digital Marketing in India

- **Case Study:**

The digital marketing landscape in India has experienced exponential growth over the past decade. With the increasing penetration of smartphones and affordable internet, businesses have shifted their focus to digital platforms to reach a broader audience. Companies like Zomato, Swiggy, and Nykaa have leveraged social media platforms, search engine optimization (SEO), and influencer marketing to create a significant impact on their target markets.

Zomato, for instance, capitalized on humor and relatability in its social media campaigns to engage millennials and Gen Z. Swiggy, on the other hand, used personalized push notifications and gamification techniques, such as the Swiggy "Loot" campaign, to drive customer engagement. Meanwhile, Nykaa's influencer collaborations and tutorial-based YouTube content helped it build trust among its predominantly female audience, positioning itself as the go-to platform for cosmetics and skincare.

Despite these success stories, challenges like data privacy concerns, ad fatigue, and fierce competition from global players like Amazon and Netflix have emerged. Indian consumers are also becoming more aware of misleading advertisements, demanding transparency and authenticity in brand communication. As digital marketing evolves, brands must continuously adapt to emerging trends like artificial intelligence (AI)-driven personalization, voice search optimization, and the metaverse to stay relevant.

- **Questions:**

1. What are the key factors driving the growth of digital marketing in India?
2. How have companies like Zomato and Nykaa differentiated themselves in the competitive digital space?

3. What challenges do Indian brands face in sustaining engagement through digital marketing?

4. Discuss the role of emerging technologies like AI and voice search in shaping the future of digital marketing.

• • •

CHAPTER XLVII

Coca-Cola's Share a Coke Campaign

- **Case Study:**

In 2011, Coca-Cola launched its "Share a Coke" campaign in Australia, which later became a global phenomenon. The campaign involved replacing the Coca-Cola logo on its bottles with popular names, encouraging consumers to "share a Coke" with friends and loved ones. This personalization strategy resonated deeply with the audience, leading to increased sales and enhanced brand loyalty.

In India, Coca-Cola adapted the campaign to include common Indian names and phrases like "Bhai" (brother) and "Dost" (friend), making it culturally relevant. The campaign's success lay in its ability to connect emotionally with consumers and encourage user-generated content on social media. Many customers shared pictures of their personalized Coke bottles, creating free publicity for the brand.

However, the campaign faced criticism for excluding less common names and not addressing environmental concerns associated with single-use plastic bottles. Coca-Cola's inability to address these issues sparked debates about the brand's responsibility toward sustainable marketing.

- **Questions:**

1. What made the "Share a Coke" campaign so successful globally?
2. How did Coca-Cola localize its campaign in India to connect with the audience?
3. What lessons can brands learn from the criticism Coca-Cola faced regarding sustainability?
4. Propose strategies for making future personalized campaigns more inclusive and eco-friendly.

• • •

CHAPTER XLVIII

Patagonia: Marketing with a Purpose

71

- **Case Study:**

Patagonia, a U.S.-based outdoor apparel brand, has carved a niche for itself through purpose-driven marketing. The company's mission is to "Save Our Home Planet," and its campaigns focus on sustainability, ethical practices, and environmental activism. Unlike traditional marketing strategies that prioritize sales, Patagonia encourages customers to "Buy Less," advocating for repairing old products instead of purchasing new ones.

In 2011, Patagonia launched its "Don't Buy This Jacket" campaign, urging consumers to think twice before making unnecessary purchases. This unconventional approach created a strong emotional connection with environmentally conscious customers, boosting brand loyalty. The company also pledged 1% of its sales to environmental causes, reinforcing its commitment to sustainability.

While Patagonia's values-driven marketing has attracted a loyal customer base, it also faces challenges. Critics argue that promoting reduced consumption while selling high-priced products creates a paradox. Moreover, balancing profitability with purpose remains a constant challenge for the brand.

- **Questions:**

1. How has Patagonia's purpose-driven marketing strategy contributed to its success?
2. Discuss the challenges of balancing profitability and sustainability in marketing.
3. How does Patagonia differentiate itself from competitors in the outdoor apparel industry?
4. Suggest ways Patagonia can address the criticism of its paradoxical messaging

• • •

CHAPTER XLIX

Amazon Prime: Redefining Customer Loyalty

- **Case Study:**

Amazon Prime has revolutionized customer loyalty programs by offering a comprehensive bundle of services, including fast delivery, exclusive deals, and access to Prime Video and Music. Launched in India in 2016, the subscription-based program has become a significant revenue driver for Amazon, with millions of Indian users signing up annually.

One of the key factors behind Prime's success is its localization strategy. Amazon introduced Prime in India at a lower price compared to global markets and offered regional content on Prime Video to cater to diverse linguistic preferences. During flagship events like "Prime Day," Amazon provides exclusive deals to Prime members, incentivizing non-members to subscribe.

Despite its popularity, Prime faces challenges like increasing competition from platforms like Flipkart Plus and JioMart. Additionally, the rising cost of subscription fees may lead to customer churn, especially in price-sensitive markets like India.

- **Questions:**

1. What makes Amazon Prime's loyalty program stand out in India?
2. How does localization contribute to the success of global brands in India?
3. Discuss the potential risks of increasing subscription fees in a price-sensitive market.
4. Propose strategies to retain customers in the face of growing competition.

• • •

CHAPTER L

The Evolution of Maggi Post-Crisis

- **Case Study:**

Maggi, the instant noodle brand by Nestlé, faced one of the biggest crises in its history in 2015 when allegations of excessive lead content led to a nationwide ban in India. The brand's sales plummeted, and its reputation suffered immensely. However, through strategic marketing and communication, Maggi managed to regain its position as the market leader within two years.

Nestlé's strategy focused on transparency, engagement, and trust-building. The company emphasized rigorous quality checks and launched campaigns like "We Miss You Too" to emotionally reconnect with customers. It also leveraged digital platforms to address customer queries directly and collaborated with influencers to rebuild trust.

The crisis highlighted the importance of crisis management and the role of marketing in regaining consumer confidence. However, Maggi continues to face challenges, such as competition from healthier alternatives and evolving consumer preferences for organic and whole-grain products.

- **Questions:**

1. How did Maggi rebuild trust and reconnect with its customers post-crisis?
2. Discuss the role of emotional branding in regaining consumer confidence.
3. What lessons can marketers learn from Maggi's crisis management strategy?
4. Suggest ways Maggi can adapt to the growing demand for healthier food options.

• • •

CHAPTER LI

Apple's Event Sponsorship Strategy

- **Case Study:**

Apple is known for its sleek designs and innovative technology, but its event sponsorship strategy is an underrated aspect of its marketing approach. The company strategically sponsors high-profile events, such as the annual Worldwide Developers Conference (WWDC) and product launch events, to build excitement around its brand. Apple's events focus on creating a premium experience, reflecting the company's brand values of exclusivity and innovation.

One example is Apple's sponsorship of the Shot on iPhone competition, where users are encouraged to share their best photography using iPhones. This campaign not only promotes user engagement but also highlights the product's capabilities. By associating with such events, Apple solidifies its position as a leader in technology and creativity.

However, Apple faces criticism for its selective sponsorship approach, which often excludes smaller communities and causes. Some argue that a broader sponsorship strategy could enhance Apple's global appeal.

- **Questions:**

1. How does Apple's event sponsorship strategy align with its brand image?
2. Discuss the role of user-generated content in Apple's marketing campaigns.
3. What are the advantages and limitations of Apple's selective sponsorship strategy?
4. Propose ways Apple can expand its sponsorship efforts to appeal to a wider audience.

• • •

CHAPTER LII

The Rise of D2C Brands in India

- **Case Study:**

Direct-to-Consumer (D2C) brands have disrupted traditional retail and e-commerce models in India. Companies like Mamaearth, Boat, and Lenskart have used digital-first strategies to establish a direct relationship with consumers, cutting out intermediaries and focusing on personalized experiences. Mamaearth, for instance, leveraged its "toxins-free" positioning to attract eco-conscious millennials. Similarly, Boat's affordable, stylish audio products targeted Gen Z and millennials through influencer marketing and social media campaigns.

By using platforms like Instagram and Facebook, these brands build strong connections with their audience. Personalization, quick feedback loops, and data-driven decision-making have been at the core of their strategies. These brands also collaborate with e-commerce platforms like Amazon while simultaneously investing in their websites and apps to enhance the consumer journey.

- **Questions:**

1. What challenges do D2C brands face in scaling operations?
2. How do D2C brands effectively use social media to engage customers?
3. Discuss the importance of consumer feedback in shaping D2C products.
4. What strategies should D2C brands adopt to compete with established FMCG giants?

• • •

CHAPTER LIII

The Success of Amul's Branding Strategy

- **Case Study:**

Amul, India's largest dairy brand, has maintained its market dominance for decades through effective branding and innovation. The "Utterly Butterly Delicious" campaign, featuring the Amul Girl, is one of the longest-running advertising campaigns in the world. The brand's ability to create topical content on current events has kept it relevant.

Amul's cooperative model ensures that it sources milk directly from farmers, maintaining quality and fair pricing. The brand has also diversified its product portfolio, entering categories like ice cream, cheese, and chocolates. Despite competition from global giants, Amul continues to dominate, leveraging affordability, trust, and innovative marketing.

- **Questions:**

1. How does Amul's cooperative model contribute to its success?
2. Analyze the impact of topical advertising on Amul's brand image.
3. What challenges does Amul face from international dairy brands?
4. How can Amul leverage digital marketing to attract younger consumers?

• • •

CHAPTER LIV

Zomato's Content Marketing Strategy

77

- **Case Study:**

Zomato, a food delivery giant, is as much a content marketing company as it is a logistics business. Known for its quirky, humorous, and relatable posts on social media, Zomato's engagement strategies have set it apart from competitors. Its "Food for Thought" campaign and regionalized content resonate with India's diverse population.

Zomato also leverages influencer marketing and user-generated content, such as reviews and food photography. By combining customer insights with data analytics, Zomato personalizes the user experience, ensuring higher retention rates. However, challenges like rising delivery costs and competition from Swiggy persist.

- **Questions:**

1. What role does personalization play in Zomato's customer retention?
2. How can Zomato sustain its content marketing success?
3. Discuss the impact of influencer marketing on food delivery platforms.
4. What strategies can Zomato adopt to reduce operational costs?

• • •

CHAPTER LV

Tata Tea's "Jaago Re" Campaign

- **Case Study:**

Tata Tea's "Jaago Re" campaign exemplifies socially responsible marketing. The campaign's focus on awakening social consciousness among consumers has included themes like voting, gender equality, and climate change. By tying its product with a cause, Tata Tea successfully created an emotional connection with consumers.

The campaign was promoted through TV, digital media, and on-ground activities. Tata Tea's ability to integrate social messages with marketing has strengthened its brand equity and differentiated it in a competitive market.

- **Questions:**

1. How does cause marketing impact brand perception?
2. Analyze the effectiveness of Tata Tea's multi-channel promotion strategy.
3. What risks do brands face when engaging in cause marketing?
4. How can Tata Tea further expand its "Jaago Re" campaign?

• • •

CHAPTER LVI

Flipkart's Big Billion Days Sale

79

- **Case Study:**

Flipkart's Big Billion Days Sale has become one of the most anticipated e-commerce events in India. The sale, launched in 2014, has leveraged heavy discounts, exclusive product launches, and strategic partnerships to drive massive consumer engagement.

The event's success is attributed to extensive digital marketing, influencer tie-ups, and gamified shopping experiences. Flipkart's logistical innovations, such as faster delivery and warehouse expansions, ensure seamless operations. However, criticisms regarding inflated pre-sale prices and supply chain bottlenecks persist.

- **Questions:**

1. How do flash sales impact consumer buying behavior?
2. Discuss the logistics challenges during large-scale e-commerce events.
3. What ethical considerations should Flipkart address during its sales?
4. How can Flipkart improve customer loyalty beyond sales events?

• • •

CHAPTER LVII

Patanjali's Rapid Growth in the FMCG Sector

- **Case Study:**

Patanjali disrupted India's FMCG market with its focus on Ayurvedic and natural products. Led by Baba Ramdev, the brand capitalized on the "Made in India" sentiment and growing health consciousness. Its extensive product portfolio includes food, personal care, and wellness items.

Patanjali's aggressive pricing strategy and widespread distribution network helped it capture market share quickly. However, challenges like quality concerns and competition from established players like Dabur and HUL threaten its growth.

- **Questions:**

1. What role did nationalism play in Patanjali's success?
2. How can Patanjali address quality control issues?
3. Discuss the impact of price wars on the FMCG sector.
4. What strategies should Patanjali adopt to sustain its growth?

• • •

CHAPTER LVIII

The Evolution of Airbnb's Marketing

81

- **Case Study:**

Airbnb revolutionized the hospitality industry by connecting travelers with unique, local experiences. The brand's marketing emphasizes belonging and community. Campaigns like "Live There" and "Made Possible by Hosts" highlight authentic travel experiences.

Airbnb's digital marketing strategy includes targeted ads, user-generated content, and partnerships with travel influencers. However, challenges like regulatory issues and competition from hotel chains persist.

- **Questions:**

1. How does user-generated content enhance Airbnb's marketing efforts?
2. Discuss the impact of regulatory challenges on Airbnb's operations.
3. What role does digital marketing play in Airbnb's growth?
4. How can Airbnb compete with traditional hotel chains?

• • •

CHAPTER LIX

Cadbury's Emotional Advertising

- **Case Study:**

Cadbury has consistently used emotional advertising to connect with Indian consumers. Campaigns like "Kuch Meetha Ho Jaaye" and "Shubh Aarambh" associate the brand with celebrations and everyday joy. The brand's use of nostalgia and local cultural nuances has strengthened its market position.

Cadbury's digital campaigns, such as the "Heartwarming Stories" series, further build emotional resonance. However, health-conscious trends and competition from premium chocolate brands pose challenges.

- **Questions:**

1. How does emotional advertising influence consumer behavior?
2. Analyze the cultural relevance of Cadbury's campaigns in India.
3. What strategies should Cadbury adopt to address health-conscious consumers?
4. How can Cadbury differentiate itself from premium chocolate brands?

• • •

CHAPTER LX

The IPL's Marketing Machine

- **Case Study:**

The Indian Premier League (IPL) is not just a cricket tournament but a marketing phenomenon. Franchises attract sponsorships from top brands, and digital platforms like Hotstar monetize viewership through subscriptions and advertisements.

IPL's marketing integrates celebrity endorsements, fan engagement, and regional content to maximize reach. However, issues like player fatigue and oversaturation could impact its future.

- **Questions:**

1. What makes IPL an effective platform for brand promotion?
2. How does regional content contribute to IPL's success?
3. Discuss the challenges of sustaining audience interest in IPL.
4. What strategies can IPL adopt to innovate its marketing?

• • •

CHAPTER LXI

The Impact of Influencer Marketing on Consumer Behavior

- **Case Study:**

In recent years, influencer marketing has become a pivotal strategy for brands to connect with their target audience. Influencers, who are individuals with significant online followings, leverage their platforms to promote products and services. This form of marketing often relies on the authenticity and relatability of influencers, as they are perceived as more trustworthy than traditional advertisements.

For instance, a skincare brand might collaborate with a beauty influencer to showcase a product's effectiveness through tutorials and reviews. Consumers, especially younger audiences, are more likely to trust and purchase products recommended by influencers they follow.

However, this approach is not without challenges. Issues such as fake followers, lack of transparency in sponsored posts, and over-commercialization can undermine the credibility of influencer marketing. Despite these challenges, the industry continues to grow, with global spending on influencer marketing projected to increase significantly.

- **Questions:**

1. How does influencer marketing differ from traditional advertising methods?
2. What are the key factors that make influencer marketing effective?
3. Discuss the potential risks associated with relying heavily on influencer marketing.
4. How can brands ensure transparency and authenticity in their influencer campaigns?

• • •

CHAPTER LXII

The Role of Data Analytics in Personalizing Marketing Campaigns

- **Case Study:**

Data analytics has revolutionized how businesses approach marketing. By leveraging consumer data, companies can create highly personalized campaigns that resonate with their target audience. For example, an e-commerce platform might analyze a customer's browsing and purchase history to recommend products they are likely to buy.

Such personalization enhances the customer experience, increasing engagement and driving sales. However, it also raises ethical concerns about data privacy and security. Businesses must navigate these challenges by adopting transparent practices and complying with regulations like the GDPR.

The success of data-driven marketing often depends on the quality of data and the sophistication of analytical tools used. Companies that invest in advanced analytics and machine learning gain a competitive edge, as they can predict trends and consumer behavior with greater accuracy.

- **Questions:**

1. What are the advantages of using data analytics in marketing?
2. Discuss the ethical implications of collecting and using consumer data.
3. How can businesses balance personalization with data privacy?
4. What role do machine learning and AI play in enhancing data-driven marketing?

• • •

CHAPTER LXIII

The Effectiveness of Emotional Branding

- **Case Study:**

Emotional branding focuses on creating strong emotional connections between a brand and its consumers. By appealing to feelings such as happiness, nostalgia, or trust, companies aim to foster loyalty and differentiate themselves from competitors.

Consider a brand like Coca-Cola, which consistently uses themes of happiness and togetherness in its campaigns. These emotional appeals resonate with audiences, making the brand more memorable and relatable. Similarly, non-profit organizations often use emotional storytelling to inspire donations and support.

While emotional branding can be powerful, it must be authentic. Brands that overuse emotional appeals risk appearing insincere, which can erode trust.

- **Questions:**

1. How does emotional branding influence consumer loyalty?
2. What are some successful examples of emotional branding?
3. Discuss the potential pitfalls of relying on emotional appeals in marketing.
4. How can brands measure the effectiveness of emotional branding?

• • •

CHAPTER LXIV

The Rise of Sustainability in Marketing

87

- **Case Study:**

Sustainability has become a crucial factor for consumers, influencing their purchasing decisions. Brands that emphasize environmentally friendly practices and products are increasingly appealing to eco-conscious audiences.

For instance, companies like Patagonia and Tesla have built their brand identity around sustainability. Patagonia's commitment to ethical sourcing and Tesla's focus on renewable energy exemplify how brands can align their marketing strategies with environmental values.

However, there is also the risk of greenwashing, where companies exaggerate or falsely claim eco-friendly practices. To maintain credibility, brands must ensure their sustainability efforts are genuine and transparent.

- **Questions:**

1. Why is sustainability important in modern marketing?
2. Discuss the concept of greenwashing and its impact on consumer trust.
3. How can companies effectively communicate their sustainability efforts?
4. What role does consumer awareness play in promoting sustainable marketing?

• • •

CHAPTER LXV

The Shift to Omnichannel Marketing

- **Case Study:**

Omnichannel marketing integrates various online and offline channels to provide a seamless customer experience. This approach recognizes that modern consumers interact with brands across multiple touchpoints, such as websites, social media, and physical stores.

A clothing retailer might allow customers to browse products online, try them in-store, and complete the purchase through a mobile app. By synchronizing these channels, the brand ensures consistency and convenience for the customer.

Despite its advantages, implementing an omnichannel strategy can be complex and resource-intensive. Businesses must invest in technology and training to align their operations.

- **Questions:**

1. What are the key components of an omnichannel marketing strategy?
2. How does omnichannel marketing enhance the customer experience?
3. Discuss the challenges businesses face when adopting omnichannel marketing.
4. How can brands measure the success of their omnichannel efforts?

• • •

CHAPTER LXVI

The Impact of User-Generated Content (UGC) on Brand Engagement

- **Case Study:**

User-generated content, such as customer reviews, social media posts, and testimonials, has become a valuable marketing tool. UGC not only provides social proof but also fosters community engagement.

Brands often encourage customers to share their experiences by hosting contests or creating branded hashtags. For example, Starbucks' #RedCupContest invites users to showcase their creativity, resulting in authentic content that promotes the brand.

While UGC is cost-effective, it requires monitoring to ensure that the content aligns with the brand's values. Negative or inappropriate content can pose reputational risks.

- **Questions:**

1. What makes user-generated content effective in marketing?
2. How can brands encourage and curate quality UGC?
3. Discuss the potential risks of relying on UGC.
4. How can businesses measure the ROI of UGC campaigns?

• • •

CHAPTER LXVII

The Role of Augmented Reality (AR) in Enhancing Customer Experiences

- **Case Study:**

Augmented reality is transforming how brands engage with consumers. By integrating AR into marketing, businesses can offer immersive experiences that bridge the gap between digital and physical worlds.

For example, IKEA's AR app allows customers to visualize furniture in their homes before purchasing. Similarly, beauty brands use AR filters to let users try on makeup virtually. These applications not only enhance convenience but also reduce purchase hesitation.

However, AR implementation requires significant investment and technological expertise. Brands must also consider accessibility to ensure that their AR features are widely usable.

- **Questions:**

1. What are the advantages of using AR in marketing?
2. Discuss the challenges brands face when adopting AR technology.
3. How can AR influence consumer purchase decisions?
4. What industries can benefit the most from AR marketing?

• • •

CHAPTER LXVIII

The Importance of Storytelling in Marketing

- **Case Study:**

Storytelling is a timeless marketing strategy that humanizes brands and captivates audiences. A compelling story can evoke emotions, convey values, and differentiate a brand from competitors.

For example, Nike's "Just Do It" campaign often features stories of resilience and determination, resonating with a wide audience. By focusing on the human element, brands can create deeper connections with their consumers.

However, successful storytelling requires authenticity and alignment with the brand's identity. Overly contrived or inconsistent narratives can backfire.

- **Questions:**

1. Why is storytelling an effective marketing tool?
2. What elements make a brand story compelling?
3. How can brands ensure their storytelling remains authentic?
4. Discuss examples of brands that have successfully used storytelling in their campaigns.

• • •

CHAPTER LXIX

The Shift Toward Experiential Marketing

- **Case Study:**

Experiential marketing focuses on creating memorable experiences that engage consumers on a deeper level. This strategy often involves interactive events, pop-ups, or immersive brand activations.

For instance, Red Bull's sponsorship of extreme sports events showcases its brand values of energy and adventure. Such experiences not only enhance brand visibility but also foster emotional connections.

However, experiential marketing can be costly and logistically challenging. Brands must carefully plan to ensure that the experiences align with their objectives and resonate with their audience.

- **Questions:**

1. What are the benefits of experiential marketing?
2. Discuss the challenges of implementing experiential campaigns.
3. How can brands measure the success of experiential marketing efforts?
4. Provide examples of successful experiential marketing campaigns.

• • •

CHAPTER LXX

The Influence of AI-Powered Chatbots in Customer Service

- **Case Study:**

Artificial intelligence has revolutionized customer service through the use of chatbots. These virtual assistants provide instant responses to customer queries, enhancing convenience and efficiency.

For example, e-commerce platforms use chatbots to assist with product recommendations, order tracking, and issue resolution. By automating routine tasks, chatbots allow businesses to allocate resources to more complex customer needs.

However, chatbot implementation must balance automation with a human touch. Over-reliance on AI can lead to impersonal interactions, frustrating customers.

- **Questions:**

1. What are the advantages of using chatbots in customer service?
2. Discuss the limitations of AI-powered.

• • •

HR

CHAPTER LXXI

Performance Management at XYZ Corporation

- **Case Study:**

XYZ Corporation is a mid-sized IT company known for its innovative products and services. Despite its technical success, the company has been facing significant challenges in managing employee performance. In the past year, turnover rates increased by 15%, and employee satisfaction scores dropped by 20%.

The performance appraisal system at XYZ Corporation was outdated. The current system relied heavily on annual reviews, which employees perceived as biased and disconnected from their actual contributions. Managers, overwhelmed with their operational responsibilities, often failed to provide constructive feedback. Moreover, the criteria for evaluating performance were not standardized, leading to inconsistencies and perceptions of favoritism.

John Carter, the newly appointed HR Director, was tasked with overhauling the performance management system. After conducting a thorough analysis, he proposed implementing a continuous performance management system. This system would include regular check-ins between managers and employees, goal setting aligned with organizational objectives, and the incorporation of 360-degree feedback.

Despite these improvements, resistance emerged. Managers argued that frequent check-ins would increase their workload, while employees worried about the potential misuse of 360-degree feedback. To address these concerns, John organized training sessions for managers and town hall meetings with employees to clarify the purpose and benefits of the new system.

Six months after implementation, XYZ Corporation reported a 10% increase in employee satisfaction and a 5% improvement in productivity metrics. However, challenges such as ensuring consistent feedback quality and monitoring the system's long-term effectiveness persisted.

- **Questions:**

1. What were the key challenges in XYZ Corporation's original performance management system?
2. How can the HR team ensure the new system remains effective over time?
3. Evaluate the use of 360-degree feedback in performance management. What are its pros and cons?
4. Suggest additional measures XYZ Corporation could take to address resistance from employees and managers.

• • •

CHAPTER LXXII

Diversity and Inclusion at ABC Global

- **Case Study:**

ABC Global, a multinational organization operating in 15 countries, prides itself on its diverse workforce. However, a recent internal survey revealed significant gaps in inclusivity. Female employees, especially in leadership roles, reported feeling undervalued. Similarly, employees from minority groups expressed concerns about a lack of career growth opportunities.

The HR department, led by Priya Mehta, initiated a comprehensive diversity and inclusion (D&I) program. The program's objectives included increasing representation in leadership roles, addressing unconscious bias, and fostering an inclusive work environment.

The first step was to revise recruitment policies to eliminate bias. Blind resume screening and structured interviews were introduced to ensure fair assessments. Leadership development programs specifically targeted underrepresented groups to prepare them for senior roles.

To tackle unconscious bias, the HR team rolled out mandatory training workshops for all employees. These workshops included interactive sessions, real-life scenarios, and tools for identifying and mitigating bias in decision-making processes.

Despite these efforts, some employees were skeptical about the initiatives, viewing them as tokenism. Priya addressed these concerns by emphasizing the organization's commitment to long-term cultural change. Quarterly updates on D&I progress were shared with the workforce, fostering transparency and trust.

A year later, the proportion of women in leadership roles increased by 15%, and employee engagement surveys reflected improved satisfaction levels among minority groups. While progress was evident, Priya acknowledged that fostering inclusion is an ongoing journey requiring continuous effort and adaptation.

- **Questions:**

1. Identify the main challenges faced by ABC Global in implementing its D&I program.
2. How effective are mandatory unconscious bias training programs in driving cultural change?
3. What additional strategies can be employed to address skepticism about D&I initiatives?
4. Discuss the role of leadership in sustaining a diverse and inclusive workplace.

• • •

CHAPTER LXXIII

Employee Engagement at DEF Retail

- **Case Study:**

DEF Retail, a nationwide retail chain, experienced a decline in employee engagement over the past two years. High workloads, limited career advancement opportunities, and inadequate recognition were frequently cited in employee feedback.

In response, the HR team, led by Sarah Nguyen, launched a multi-faceted engagement strategy. Key initiatives included:

1. **Recognition Programs:** Monthly awards for high performers, peer recognition platforms, and instant rewards for exceptional contributions.
2. **Career Development:** Introduction of mentorship programs, skill enhancement workshops, and clear pathways for internal promotions.
3. **Work-Life Balance:** Flexible work schedules and increased access to mental health resources.

To ensure transparency, Sarah established employee engagement committees in every branch. These committees served as a platform for employees to voice their concerns and contribute to policy-making.

Initial feedback was promising, with employees appreciating the improved recognition systems and flexible schedules. However, challenges remained. Some employees felt the mentorship programs were poorly implemented, while others highlighted inconsistent practices across branches.

DEF Retail's leadership acknowledged these issues and committed to refining the programs. By fostering a culture of continuous improvement and open communication, the organization aimed to sustain employee engagement in the long term.

- **Questions:**

1. What factors contributed to the decline in employee engagement at DEF Retail?
2. Evaluate the effectiveness of the strategies implemented by Sarah Nguyen.
3. How can DEF Retail address the inconsistencies in program implementation across branches?
4. Suggest additional measures to enhance employee engagement.

• • •

CHAPTER LXXIV

Training and Development at GHI Manufacturing

- **Case Study:**

GHI Manufacturing is a leading producer of industrial equipment, employing over 5,000 workers globally. Despite its strong market position, the company faced issues with skill gaps among its workforce, particularly as new technologies were introduced on the production floor. This led to decreased productivity and a rise in workplace errors.

The HR department, headed by Mark Peterson, decided to implement a robust training and development program. The program's goals included upskilling employees, improving productivity, and reducing errors. It consisted of the following components:

1. **Technical Training**: Hands-on workshops on the latest machinery and production techniques.
2. **Soft Skills Development**: Programs focused on communication, teamwork, and problem-solving.
3. **E-Learning Platforms**: Access to online courses and certifications to promote continuous learning.

To motivate employees, the company linked training participation to performance appraisals and career progression opportunities. However, challenges emerged. Older employees were reluctant to adopt new learning methods, while younger employees expressed concerns about the training's relevance to their career goals.

Mark addressed these issues by introducing mentorship programs where experienced workers guided newer employees. He also conducted surveys to tailor training content to employee needs. Six months after launching the program, GHI Manufacturing reported a 20% increase in productivity and a 15% reduction in errors. However, Mark recognized the need for ongoing evaluation to adapt the program to future challenges.

- **Questions:**

1. What were the main challenges faced by GHI Manufacturing in upskilling its workforce?
2. How effective was the training program in addressing the company's skill gaps?
3. Discuss the role of mentorship programs in enhancing training outcomes.
4. Suggest additional measures to make the training program more effective and inclusive.

• • •

CHAPTER LXXV

Workplace Conflict Resolution at JKL Services

- **Case Study:**

JKL Services, a mid-sized consulting firm, experienced increasing workplace conflicts as the company expanded its operations. These conflicts ranged from inter-departmental disagreements to personal clashes between team members. Surveys revealed that unresolved conflicts were negatively impacting morale and productivity.

The HR team, led by Elena Garcia, introduced a conflict resolution framework to address these issues. Key elements of the framework included:

1. **Conflict Resolution Training:** Workshops for employees and managers on effective communication and mediation techniques.
2. **Mediation Committees:** Establishing neutral committees to resolve disputes fairly and transparently.
3. **Anonymous Reporting:** Creating channels for employees to report conflicts without fear of retaliation.

Elena also emphasized the importance of a positive organizational culture. Regular team-building activities and open forums were introduced to foster collaboration and mutual respect.

While the framework showed initial success, challenges persisted. Some employees hesitated to report conflicts due to a lack of trust in the system, and managers struggled to balance conflict resolution responsibilities with their regular duties.

To address these issues, Elena focused on building trust through consistent communication and follow-up on reported cases. Within a year, employee surveys indicated a 25% improvement in workplace relationships and a 10% increase in productivity.

- **Questions:**

1. What were the key factors contributing to workplace conflicts at JKL Services?
2. Evaluate the effectiveness of the conflict resolution framework introduced by Elena Garcia.
3. How can JKL Services further build trust in its conflict resolution system?
4. Suggest additional strategies to prevent workplace conflicts in the future.

• • •

CHAPTER LXXVI

Employee Retention at TechNova Solutions

- **Background:**

TechNova Solutions, a mid-sized IT company, has been facing a high attrition rate over the past two years. The company operates in a competitive industry where employee retention is critical due to the high cost of replacing skilled workers. TechNova prides itself on providing competitive salaries, flexible work hours, and a modern office environment. However, exit interviews reveal that employees often leave for better career growth opportunities, dissatisfaction with leadership, and lack of recognition for their efforts.

- **The Problem:**

The HR team identified that most resignations occur within the first three years of employment. Despite offering salary hikes and benefits, the attrition rate has remained above 20%, which is higher than the industry average. The issue is impacting project delivery timelines, client satisfaction, and overall team morale.

- **HR Initiatives:**

In response, TechNova's HR team introduced several initiatives to improve employee retention:

1. **Mentorship Programs:** Assigning senior employees as mentors to help new hires navigate their roles and build relationships.
2. **Career Growth Plans:** Creating clear career paths and providing upskilling opportunities through workshops and certifications.
3. **Employee Recognition:** Launching a monthly "Star Performer" award and offering public recognition in team meetings.
4. **Leadership Training:** Conducting workshops for managers to improve their leadership and communication skills.

5. **Work-Life Balance:** Introducing mental health programs and wellness initiatives to support employees' well-being.

- **Outcome:**

Six months after implementing these initiatives, the HR team conducted an internal survey. While 80% of employees appreciated the new recognition programs and career growth plans, some still expressed concerns about the leadership style in certain departments. The attrition rate dropped to 15%, but retaining employees beyond the three-year mark remained a challenge.

- **Questions:**

1. What additional steps can TechNova take to further reduce its attrition rate?
2. How can the HR team address concerns related to leadership in certain departments?
3. Evaluate the effectiveness of the implemented initiatives and suggest improvements.
4. Should TechNova consider revising its hiring strategy to focus on cultural fit? Why or why not?
5. How can mentorship programs be further strengthened to ensure long-term employee engagement?

• • •

CHAPTER LXXVII

Diversity and Inclusion at Bright Horizons

- **Background:**

Bright Horizons is a leading global consulting firm known for its innovative solutions. However, the company has faced criticism for its lack of diversity, particularly in leadership roles. Out of 20 senior executives, only two are women, and none represent minority groups. Employees have voiced concerns about unconscious bias and limited opportunities for underrepresented groups.

- **The Problem:**

The HR team conducted a diversity audit and found that while Bright Horizons' recruitment strategy focused on hiring the best talent, there was little emphasis on diversity. Additionally, many employees felt that the company's culture did not support open dialogue about inclusion.

- **HR Initiatives:**

The HR department launched a comprehensive Diversity and Inclusion (D&I) program, which included:

1. **Diversity Targets:** Setting clear goals to increase representation of women and minority groups at all levels.
2. **Bias Training:** Conducting workshops to raise awareness about unconscious bias among employees and managers.
3. **Employee Resource Groups (ERGs):** Creating ERGs for women, LGBTQ+ employees, and minority groups to foster a sense of community.
4. **Mentorship Programs:** Pairing underrepresented employees with senior leaders to support career development.
5. **Transparent Hiring Processes:** Implementing structured interviews to reduce bias and ensure equal opportunities.

- **Outcome:**

One year later, Bright Horizons reported a 10% increase in the hiring of diverse candidates. The ERGs became popular, with over 40% of employees participating. However, progress in promoting diverse leaders remained slow. Some employees felt the initiatives were more symbolic than impactful.

- **Questions:**

1. How can Bright Horizons ensure that its D&I initiatives lead to meaningful cultural change?
2. What measures can the company take to accelerate the promotion of diverse leaders?
3. Evaluate the role of ERGs in creating an inclusive workplace and suggest ways to enhance their effectiveness.
4. How can Bright Horizons balance merit-based hiring with diversity goals?
5. What additional steps can be taken to address unconscious bias in the workplace?

• • •

CHAPTER LXXVIII

Managing Remote Teams at GlobalTech

- **Background:**

GlobalTech, an international software company, transitioned to remote work during the COVID-19 pandemic. While the initial shift was smooth, the company soon faced challenges in maintaining productivity, collaboration, and employee engagement. Managers reported difficulties in monitoring performance, and employees felt isolated and disconnected from their teams.

- **The Problem:**

The HR team conducted a survey to understand the challenges of remote work. Key findings included:

1. Lack of effective communication between teams.
2. Increased feelings of burnout and stress among employees.
3. Difficulty in managing work-life balance.
4. Limited opportunities for team bonding and collaboration.

- **HR Initiatives:**

To address these issues, GlobalTech's HR team introduced the following measures:

1. **Regular Check-Ins:** Encouraging managers to conduct weekly one-on-one meetings with team members.
2. **Virtual Team Building:** Organizing online games, workshops, and social events to foster team bonding.
3. **Mental Health Support:** Providing access to counseling services and hosting webinars on stress management.
4. **Flexible Schedules:** Allowing employees to choose their working hours to balance personal and professional responsibilities.

5. **Clear Communication Channels:** Implementing tools like Slack and Microsoft Teams to streamline communication.

- **Outcome:**

Within six months, employee satisfaction scores improved by 20%. Many employees appreciated the flexible schedules and mental health initiatives. However, some teams continued to struggle with collaboration, especially in cross-functional projects.

- **Questions:**

1. What additional steps can GlobalTech take to improve collaboration in remote teams?
2. How can managers ensure fair performance evaluations for remote employees?
3. Evaluate the effectiveness of virtual team-building activities and suggest improvements.
4. Should GlobalTech consider a hybrid work model? Why or why not?
5. How can the HR team address feelings of isolation among remote employees?

• • •

CHAPTER LXXIX

Talent Acquisition Challenges at Apex Enterprises

- **Background:**

Apex Enterprises, a fast-growing manufacturing company, has been struggling to attract top talent. Despite offering competitive salaries and benefits, the company's recruitment process is lengthy, and its brand presence is weak compared to competitors. Feedback from candidates who declined job offers highlighted concerns about delayed responses, lack of clarity during interviews, and limited career advancement opportunities.

- **The Problem:**

The HR team realized that the traditional methods of recruitment—posting on job boards and relying on referrals—were no longer effective. Additionally, the lack of a strong employer brand made it difficult to compete for talent in a saturated job market.

- **HR Initiatives:**

To tackle these challenges, Apex Enterprises implemented the following measures:

1. **Streamlined Recruitment Process:** Reducing the time-to-hire by automating initial screening and scheduling interviews efficiently.
2. **Employer Branding Campaigns:** Enhancing the company's online presence through social media, employee testimonials, and participation in industry events.
3. **Campus Recruitment Drives:** Building relationships with universities to attract fresh talent.
4. **Employee Referral Program:** Offering incentives to employees for successful referrals.

5. **Comprehensive Onboarding:** Creating a structured onboarding program to ensure new hires feel welcomed and aligned with company values.

- **Outcome:**

Within a year, Apex Enterprises saw a 30% increase in job applications. Candidate satisfaction scores improved, with many appreciating the quicker hiring process and better communication. However, the company still faced challenges in attracting experienced professionals for niche roles.

- **Questions:**

1. How can Apex Enterprises further enhance its employer brand to attract experienced professionals?
2. What additional steps can the HR team take to improve the candidate experience?
3. Evaluate the effectiveness of campus recruitment drives in meeting the company's talent needs.
4. Should Apex Enterprises focus more on upskilling internal talent to fill niche roles? Why or why not?
5. How can technology be leveraged to make the recruitment process more efficient?

• • •

CHAPTER LXXX

Managing Employee Turnover at XYZ Technologies

- **Background**

XYZ Technologies, a mid-sized IT company based in Bengaluru, has experienced rapid growth over the past five years. Despite its success, the organization faces a critical issue: high employee turnover. The HR department observed that nearly 25% of employees leave within their first two years of employment. This has not only increased recruitment costs but also affected project timelines and client satisfaction.

To address this, the HR team conducted exit interviews to identify common reasons for turnover. The findings revealed three key issues: lack of career growth opportunities, dissatisfaction with compensation, and work-life imbalance due to excessive workloads. Additionally, employee engagement surveys highlighted that many employees felt undervalued and disconnected from the company's vision.

The HR manager, Priya Sharma, proposed a multi-pronged approach to tackle the issue. First, the company introduced a structured career development program that included mentorship, training, and regular performance appraisals to help employees grow within the organization. Second, compensation packages were reviewed and revised to align with industry standards, along with the introduction of non-monetary benefits such as flexible working hours, remote work options, and wellness programs. Third, team-building activities and regular town halls were implemented to improve communication and foster a sense of belonging.

Six months later, XYZ Technologies conducted another employee engagement survey and observed a 20% improvement in satisfaction scores. However, Priya noticed that turnover rates had only marginally reduced, from 25% to 22%. She now faces a dilemma: whether to continue with the current initiatives or explore other strategies to further reduce turnover.

- **Questions:**

1. What additional steps can Priya Sharma take to address employee turnover at XYZ Technologies?
2. How can the HR team measure the effectiveness of the current initiatives?
3. What role does leadership play in improving employee retention?
4. Suggest ways to align company policies with employee expectations to foster long-term loyalty.

• • •

CHAPTER LXXXI

Diversity and Inclusion at Alpha Finance

- **Background:**

Alpha Finance, a leading financial services firm in Mumbai, has prided itself on being an equal opportunity employer. However, a recent internal audit revealed significant gaps in diversity at the senior management level. While the company's workforce is 40% female, only 5% of leadership roles are held by women. Similarly, employees from minority communities and differently-abled individuals are underrepresented across departments.

Recognizing the importance of diversity and inclusion (D&I) in fostering innovation and better decision-making, the CEO, Arjun Mehta, tasked the HR team with developing a comprehensive D&I strategy. The HR head, Shweta Verma, initiated a series of measures, including unconscious bias training for managers, targeted recruitment drives, and mentorship programs for women and underrepresented groups. Additionally, an employee resource group (ERG) was established to provide a platform for discussions and support around diversity issues.

Despite these efforts, Shweta encountered resistance from some senior managers who felt that the focus on diversity might compromise merit-based hiring. Moreover, some employees expressed skepticism about the company's commitment to D&I, perceiving the initiatives as superficial.

To address these challenges, Shweta launched a communication campaign to highlight the business case for diversity, showcasing examples of how diverse teams had driven success in other organizations. She also collaborated with external experts to refine the company's hiring and promotion processes to ensure they were both inclusive and merit-based.

- **Questions:**

1. What strategies can Alpha Finance adopt to overcome resistance to D&I initiatives?
2. How can Shweta ensure the long-term sustainability of the company's D&I programs?

3. What metrics should the HR team track to evaluate the success of the D&I strategy?
4. How can the company address employee skepticism about its commitment to diversity?

• • •

CHAPTER LXXXII

Managing Remote Work Challenges at Stellar Enterprises

- **Background:**

Stellar Enterprises, a leading e-commerce company, transitioned to remote work during the COVID-19 pandemic. While employees appreciated the flexibility, HR surveys revealed emerging challenges such as feelings of isolation, communication gaps, and difficulties in maintaining work-life balance. Managers also reported a decline in team collaboration and innovation.

The HR team, led by Rohan Kapoor, implemented several initiatives to address these issues. Virtual team-building activities were organized to foster camaraderie, and managers were trained on maintaining regular check-ins with their teams. To promote work-life balance, the company introduced mandatory offline hours and encouraged employees to take mental health leaves when needed.

Despite these efforts, productivity levels remained inconsistent, with some teams excelling while others struggled. Employees also expressed concerns about limited career visibility and professional growth opportunities in a remote setting. Senior leaders debated whether to continue remote work, return to the office, or adopt a hybrid model.

- **Questions:**

1. What are the advantages and disadvantages of adopting a hybrid work model for Stellar Enterprises?
2. How can HR address the career growth concerns of remote employees?
3. What additional measures can Stellar Enterprises take to improve team collaboration in a remote setting?
4. How can the company ensure consistent productivity across teams?

• • •

CHAPTER LXXXIII

Resolving Workplace Conflict at GreenLeaf Industries

- **Case Study:**

GreenLeaf Industries, an agro-based company in Gujarat, faced a workplace conflict that disrupted team dynamics. Two senior managers, Rakesh and Neha, had a disagreement over resource allocation for their respective projects. The conflict escalated, leading to strained relationships within their teams and delays in project delivery.

The HR manager, Sunita Joshi, intervened to mediate the situation. She conducted individual meetings with Rakesh and Neha to understand their perspectives and facilitated a joint discussion to find common ground. Sunita proposed a compromise: reallocating resources based on project priorities and setting up a system for transparent communication between departments.

While the immediate conflict was resolved, Sunita realized that underlying issues such as unclear roles and responsibilities, lack of communication, and competition for resources could lead to future disputes. She decided to implement conflict resolution training for managers and create a cross-functional task force to improve collaboration.

- **Questions:**

1. How can HR proactively address the root causes of workplace conflicts at GreenLeaf Industries?
2. What role does communication play in preventing and resolving conflicts?
3. How can Sunita ensure long-term collaboration between departments?
4. Suggest ways to measure the impact of conflict resolution initiatives.

• • •

CHAPTER LXXXIV

Implementing Performance Management at Zenith Corporation

- **Background:**

Zenith Corporation, a manufacturing firm based in Pune, recently revamped its performance management system to align with organizational goals. The new system emphasizes continuous feedback, goal setting, and employee development. However, employees expressed mixed reactions to the changes. While some appreciated the focus on growth, others felt that the system's emphasis on frequent reviews created undue pressure.

The HR director, Anjali Desai, organized workshops to familiarize employees with the new system and address their concerns. Managers were trained to provide constructive feedback and support employees in achieving their goals. To further encourage transparency, a rewards and recognition program was introduced to celebrate top performers.

Despite these efforts, Anjali noticed discrepancies in how managers implemented the new system. Some provided vague feedback, while others struggled to set measurable goals. This inconsistency risked undermining the system's effectiveness.

- **Questions:**

1. What steps can Anjali take to ensure consistent implementation of the performance management system?
2. How can the HR team address employee concerns about the increased frequency of reviews?
3. What strategies can Zenith Corporation use to foster a culture of continuous feedback?
4. How can the company evaluate the success of its revamped performance management system?

• • •

CHAPTER LXXXV

Talent Acquisition and Retention in a Competitive Market

- **Background:**

FutureTech, a leading IT solutions provider in India, was struggling to attract and retain top talent in the highly competitive technology sector. Despite offering competitive salaries and benefits, the company saw a 25% turnover rate among its employees, especially those with 2-5 years of experience. Exit interviews revealed that employees left due to limited career progression opportunities, lack of skill development, and a disconnect with organizational values. To address these issues, the HR team implemented a robust talent acquisition and retention strategy.

- **Key Initiatives:**

1. **Employer Branding:** FutureTech revamped its employer brand by showcasing success stories of employees, promoting work-life balance, and emphasizing its commitment to innovation. The company also collaborated with universities to attract young talent through internships and hackathons.
2. **Skill Development Programs:** A new learning management system was introduced, offering employees access to certifications, technical courses, and leadership training. Employees who completed certifications received monetary rewards or promotions.
3. **Mentorship Program:** To address career progression concerns, a mentorship program paired junior employees with senior leaders to guide their professional growth. This also helped employees feel more connected to the organization.
4. **Workplace Flexibility:** The company introduced flexible working hours and remote work options, which improved employee satisfaction.
5. **Recognition and Rewards:** A monthly "Star Performer" program was introduced to recognize and reward exceptional employees publicly.

- **Outcome:**

Within 12 months, FutureTech reduced its turnover rate to 12%, improved employee satisfaction scores by 30%, and saw a 40% increase in applications from top-tier universities. Employees reported feeling more valued, with clear career growth opportunities and a better work-life balance.

- **Questions:**

1. What were the primary reasons for FutureTech's high turnover rate?
2. How did FutureTech's initiatives address employee concerns?
3. What role did skill development and mentorship play in reducing turnover?
4. How can FutureTech sustain these improvements in the long term?

• • •

CHAPTER LXXXVI

Managing Workplace Diversity and Inclusion

- **Background:**

Global Horizons, a multinational consultancy firm, expanded its operations to Asia and Africa, significantly diversifying its workforce. However, challenges related to cultural misunderstandings, unconscious bias, and limited communication between teams surfaced. These issues negatively impacted team cohesion and overall productivity. Realizing the need for action, the HR team developed a Diversity and Inclusion (D&I) strategy.

- **Key Initiatives:**

1. **Diversity Training:** Workshops on cultural awareness, unconscious bias, and inclusive leadership were made mandatory for all employees, including senior leaders.
2. **Employee Resource Groups (ERGs):** The company established ERGs for various employee demographics, such as women in leadership, LGBTQ+ employees, and regional cultural groups, providing safe spaces for discussion and collaboration.
3. **Inclusive Hiring Practices:** Job descriptions were rewritten to remove biased language, and hiring panels included diverse members to ensure fair recruitment.
4. **Celebrating Diversity:** The company celebrated international cultural festivals and observed awareness days to promote understanding and appreciation of different cultures.
5. **Feedback Mechanism:** An anonymous feedback system allowed employees to report discrimination or bias without fear of retaliation. These reports were addressed by a dedicated D&I team.

- **Outcome:**

Within two years, Global Horizons saw a 20% increase in employee satisfaction related to workplace culture. Collaboration across regions improved, and diverse teams reported higher innovation levels. The company also received industry awards for its D&I practices.

- **Questions:**

1. What challenges did Global Horizons face after expanding to Asia and Africa?
2. How did the D&I strategy contribute to improving workplace culture?
3. Why are employee resource groups (ERGs) important in promoting inclusion?
4. What measures can ensure the long-term success of the D&I initiatives?

• • •

CHAPTER LXXXVII

Implementing Performance Management Systems

- **Background:**

Visionary Apparel, a mid-sized garment manufacturing company, faced declining productivity and morale due to its outdated performance appraisal system. Employees complained that appraisals were inconsistent, lacked transparency, and didn't align with their goals. To address these concerns, the HR team designed a modern performance management system.

- **Key Initiatives:**

1. **Goal Setting:** Employees were encouraged to set SMART (Specific, Measurable, Achievable, Relevant, Time-bound) goals aligned with organizational objectives. Managers reviewed and approved these goals at the start of the year.
2. **Continuous Feedback:** The annual appraisal was replaced with a quarterly review system. Managers provided regular feedback, allowing employees to improve continuously.
3. **360-Degree Feedback:** Input from peers, subordinates, and supervisors was incorporated into performance evaluations to provide a holistic view of an employee's contributions.
4. **Performance-Based Rewards:** High performers received monetary bonuses, promotions, and opportunities to work on strategic projects.
5. **Training for Managers:** Workshops on effective performance management equipped managers to conduct meaningful reviews and provide constructive feedback.

- **Outcome:**

The new system resulted in a 25% increase in productivity and a 15% improvement in employee satisfaction scores. Employees appreciated the transparency and fairness of the process, while managers reported better team engagement.

- **Questions:**

1. What were the limitations of Visionary Apparel's old performance appraisal system?
2. How did SMART goals improve the performance management process?
3. What benefits did continuous and 360-degree feedback bring to the organization?
4. How can Visionary Apparel ensure consistent implementation of the new system?

• • •

Crisis Management During Layoffs

- **Background:**

TechNova, a leading electronics company, faced financial challenges during a global economic slowdown. To sustain operations, the company decided to downsize its workforce by 15%. This announcement caused panic among employees, leading to decreased productivity and trust issues. The HR team was tasked with managing the layoffs while minimizing the impact on morale.

- **Key Initiatives:**

1. **Transparent Communication:** Leaders held town hall meetings to explain the financial situation, the reasons for layoffs, and the selection criteria. They assured employees that the process would be fair and objective.
2. **Support for Affected Employees:** Laid-off employees received generous severance packages, career counseling, and outplacement services to help them find new jobs.
3. **Employee Assistance Program:** Counseling services were offered to remaining employees to address their concerns and anxieties.
4. **Rebuilding Trust:** The leadership introduced open-door policies and frequent updates on company performance to rebuild trust. Retention bonuses were offered to critical employees.

- **Outcome:**

While layoffs are never easy, TechNova managed the process with dignity and fairness. Employee satisfaction scores rebounded within six months, and productivity levels stabilized. The company's transparent approach was praised by industry analysts.

- **Questions:**

1. What challenges did TechNova face during the layoffs?
2. How did transparent communication help in managing the crisis?
3. Why is it important to support both affected and remaining employees during layoffs?
4. What additional measures could TechNova take to maintain employee trust?

• • •

CHAPTER LXXXIX

Enhancing Employee Engagement Through Gamification

- **Background:**

InspireBank, a mid-sized private bank in India, noticed declining employee engagement and motivation levels. The HR team decided to leverage gamification techniques to create a more engaging work environment and drive employee productivity.

- **Key Initiatives:**

1. **Learning and Development:** Gamified e-learning platforms were introduced, where employees earned points and badges for completing training modules and certifications.
2. **Sales Challenges:** Teams competed in friendly sales competitions with rewards for top performers. Progress was tracked using leaderboards visible to all employees.
3. **Recognition Platform:** A digital platform allowed employees to recognize and reward their peers for outstanding contributions. Points earned could be redeemed for gift cards or other perks.
4. **Wellness Programs:** Fitness challenges encouraged employees to adopt healthier lifestyles, with incentives for achieving milestones such as daily step goals or yoga sessions.

- **Outcome:**

Within a year, InspireBank's employee engagement scores increased by 40%. Sales targets were exceeded by 15%, and participation in training programs tripled. Employees reported feeling more motivated and appreciated.

- **Questions:**

1. How did gamification improve employee engagement at InspireBank?
2. What role did friendly competition play in boosting team performance?
3. Why is peer recognition important in the workplace?
4. What other areas can benefit from gamification techniques?

• • •

The Remote Work Challenge

- **Case Overview:**

XYZ Corporation, a mid-sized IT services company based in Bangalore, transitioned to a fully remote work model in early 2020 due to the COVID-19 pandemic. While initially successful, the company began facing challenges related to employee engagement, productivity, and retention. Key employees started reporting feelings of isolation, and team leaders noted a decline in collaboration and innovation. In response, HR launched initiatives such as virtual team-building activities, flexible work hours, and regular check-ins. Despite these efforts, the problems persisted, and the company's turnover rate increased by 12% in 2021.

HR decided to conduct a survey, which revealed that employees missed in-person interactions and found it difficult to maintain work-life balance while working from home. Many employees also expressed concerns about unclear communication from managers and a lack of career development opportunities.

In 2022, XYZ Corporation adopted a hybrid model, allowing employees to work from the office two days a week. While this addressed some concerns, others persisted, such as resistance from employees who had relocated and preferred full-time remote work. The HR team is now considering further policy adjustments to strike a balance between organizational goals and employee preferences.

- **Questions:**

1. What steps should HR take to improve employee engagement and reduce turnover in a hybrid work model?
2. How can XYZ Corporation address the concerns of employees who prefer full-time remote work?
3. What strategies can HR adopt to ensure effective communication and collaboration in a hybrid environment?

4. How can the company provide better career development opportunities for remote and hybrid workers?

•••

133

Diversity and Inclusion Dilemma

Case Overview:

ABC Industries, a leading manufacturing firm, prides itself on diversity and inclusion (D&I). However, a recent internal audit revealed a significant gender pay gap and underrepresentation of women and minorities in leadership roles. Additionally, a survey highlighted that many employees from diverse backgrounds felt excluded from key decision-making processes and perceived bias in promotion criteria.

In response, HR launched a series of workshops on unconscious bias and inclusive leadership for managers. The company also set a target to achieve 40% representation of women in leadership within five years. Despite these initiatives, progress has been slow, and employees remain skeptical about the organization's commitment to D&I.

The CEO has asked HR to create a detailed action plan to accelerate progress and build trust among employees. HR must address systemic barriers and ensure that D&I becomes an integral part of the company's culture.

Questions:

1. What steps can HR take to address the gender pay gap and promote equal opportunities?
2. How can the company ensure accountability for D&I goals across all levels of management?
3. What strategies can HR use to build trust and demonstrate the organization's commitment to D&I?
4. How can the company ensure sustainable progress toward its D&I objectives?

• • •

Managing Workforce Reductions

- **Case Overview:**

PQR Limited, an automobile company, faced significant financial losses due to a downturn in the market. To sustain operations, the company decided to reduce its workforce by 20%. HR faced the daunting task of managing layoffs while maintaining employee morale and protecting the company's reputation.

HR implemented a transparent communication strategy, informing employees about the financial challenges and the rationale behind the layoffs. Affected employees were offered generous severance packages, career counseling, and job placement assistance. The company also conducted town hall meetings to address employee concerns and reassure the remaining workforce.

Despite these efforts, the morale of retained employees remained low, with many expressing anxiety about job security and reduced workloads. Productivity declined, and several high-performing employees resigned within months of the layoffs.

- **Questions:**

1. How can HR support retained employees to rebuild morale and restore productivity?
2. What long-term strategies can PQR Limited adopt to prevent attrition of high-performing employees post-layoff?
3. How can the company improve its communication strategy during and after workforce reductions?
4. What lessons can HR learn from this experience to handle future downsizing more effectively?

• • •

Implementing a Performance Management System

- **Case Overview:**

STU Enterprises, a fast-growing e-commerce startup, struggled with inconsistent performance evaluation practices. Managers often relied on subjective judgments, leading to employee dissatisfaction and complaints of favoritism. To address this, HR introduced a new performance management system (PMS) that included key performance indicators (KPIs), quarterly reviews, and 360-degree feedback.

While the new PMS aimed to create transparency and fairness, its implementation faced resistance. Managers found the system time-consuming, and employees were skeptical about the confidentiality of 360-degree feedback. Additionally, technical glitches in the performance management software led to frustration among users.

HR organized training sessions to help managers and employees adapt to the system and worked with the IT team to resolve technical issues. Six months later, the company saw some improvement, but the system's effectiveness remained below expectations.

- **Questions:**

1. How can HR address resistance to the new performance management system?
2. What steps can be taken to improve the adoption and effectiveness of the PMS?
3. How can the company ensure that 360-degree feedback is used constructively and confidentially?
4. What role should managers play in driving the success of the new PMS?

• • •

The Training and Development Paradox

- **Case Overview:**

DEF Tech, a leading software development firm, invested heavily in training and development (T&D) programs to upskill its workforce. The company introduced online courses, leadership development workshops, and certifications. However, participation rates were low, especially among mid-level managers who claimed they were too busy to attend training sessions. Some employees felt that the training programs were not aligned with their career goals.

HR conducted a feedback survey, which revealed that employees preferred personalized learning paths and shorter training modules. They also wanted greater clarity on how training would impact their career progression. Based on this feedback, HR redesigned the T&D programs, incorporating micro-learning modules, gamification, and clear links to promotion criteria.

While the redesigned programs showed improved participation, some employees still viewed training as a low priority. HR is exploring further ways to enhance the impact of T&D initiatives.

- **Questions:**

1. What strategies can HR use to increase participation in training programs?
2. How can HR ensure that training aligns with employee career goals and organizational objectives?
3. What role can technology play in making T&D programs more effective and engaging?
4. How can HR demonstrate the value of training to employees and managers?

• • •

Addressing Workplace Harassment

Case Overview:

XYZ Retail faced a major crisis when multiple employees reported incidents of workplace harassment. The company's existing policies on harassment were outdated, and many employees felt unsafe reporting incidents due to fear of retaliation.

HR immediately conducted an investigation, terminating the offenders and providing support to victims. They also revised the company's anti-harassment policies and introduced mandatory training sessions on workplace behavior and reporting mechanisms. An anonymous helpline was set up to encourage employees to report issues without fear.

While these measures were well-received, rebuilding trust among employees proved challenging. Many employees felt that the company's actions were reactive rather than proactive.

Questions:

1. How can HR ensure a safe and inclusive workplace for all employees?
2. What steps can be taken to rebuild trust among employees after a harassment crisis?
3. How can HR proactively address workplace harassment before incidents occur?
4. What role does leadership play in fostering a culture of respect and accountability?

• • •

Retaining Top Talent

- **Case Overview:**

LMN Corp, a consulting firm, faced a challenge when two of its star employees left within three months. Both cited limited career advancement opportunities and a lack of recognition for their contributions as reasons for their departure. This triggered concerns about retaining other high-performing employees.

HR conducted exit interviews and identified gaps in the company's reward and recognition programs. In response, they launched a new initiative to recognize outstanding performance through monthly awards, salary hikes, and career development plans. Additionally, HR introduced mentorship programs to guide employees in their career growth.

Despite these efforts, employee turnover remained high. Some employees felt the new initiatives were superficial and failed to address systemic issues like work-life balance and workload management.

- **Questions:**

1. How can HR identify and address the root causes of employee turnover?
2. What steps should HR take to create meaningful career development opportunities for employees?
3. How can the company's reward and recognition programs be made more effective?
4. What strategies can HR adopt to improve work-life balance for employees?

• • •

Talent Retention in IT Firms

- **Background:**

GlobalTech Solutions, a leading IT services firm, has been facing a significant challenge in retaining its top talent over the past two years. With over 10,000 employees, the organization specializes in software development, IT consulting, and digital transformation services. Despite offering competitive salaries, the company's attrition rate has risen to 18%, significantly higher than the industry average of 12%. Exit interviews reveal that employees are leaving due to limited career growth opportunities, excessive workloads, and lack of recognition.

- **The Problem:**

The Human Resource department is under pressure to address these issues. The CEO, Mr. Rajesh Gupta, has emphasized the importance of retaining high-performing employees to maintain the company's competitive edge. The HR team conducted an internal survey, which revealed the following:

- 60% of employees feel their efforts are not recognized adequately.
- 45% believe there are limited growth opportunities within the organization.
- 35% cited work-life imbalance as a major concern.

The HR team has proposed initiatives such as implementing a robust recognition program, introducing flexible work hours, and enhancing internal job rotation programs. However, there are concerns about the cost implications and the practicality of these initiatives.

- **Key Questions:**

1. What steps can GlobalTech take to improve employee retention without significantly increasing costs?
2. How can the organization effectively balance workloads to improve work-life balance?
3. What role does leadership play in retaining top talent, and how can it be improved?
4. Suggest a framework for a recognition program that would be cost-effective and impactful.

• • •

Diversity and Inclusion in the Workplace

- **Background**

Bright Horizons, a multinational corporation in the consumer goods industry, prides itself on innovation and a diverse workforce. However, a recent internal audit revealed gaps in diversity at the leadership level. While 45% of the workforce comprises women, only 15% occupy senior leadership positions. Additionally, employees from minority backgrounds reported feeling underrepresented and overlooked for promotions.

- **The Problem**

The lack of diversity in leadership positions has raised concerns about unconscious bias and inequitable promotion practices. The company's CEO, Ms. Priya Mehta, has committed to addressing these issues by launching a Diversity and Inclusion (D&I) program. The proposed initiatives include mandatory bias training for managers, establishing mentorship programs for underrepresented groups, and setting diversity hiring targets. However, there is skepticism among employees about whether these initiatives will bring meaningful change.

- **Key Questions:**

1. What challenges might Bright Horizons face in implementing the D&I program, and how can they overcome them?
2. How can mentorship programs be designed to ensure their effectiveness?
3. What metrics should the company use to measure the success of its D&I initiatives?
4. Discuss the role of leadership commitment in fostering a diverse and inclusive workplace.

• • •

Managing Remote Teams

- **Background**

TechInnovate, a mid-sized software company, transitioned to remote work during the COVID-19 pandemic. While productivity initially increased, the company has recently faced challenges in managing its remote teams. Employees report feelings of isolation, reduced collaboration, and communication gaps. Managers have also struggled with monitoring performance and ensuring accountability.

- **The Problem**

To address these challenges, the HR department is considering introducing a hybrid work model, investing in collaboration tools, and organizing virtual team-building activities. However, employees have expressed mixed opinions about returning to the office. Some prefer remote work due to flexibility, while others believe in-person interactions are essential for effective collaboration.

- **Key Questions:**

1. What strategies can TechInnovate use to improve collaboration and communication in remote teams?
2. How can the company address employee isolation while maintaining a remote work model?
3. What factors should be considered while implementing a hybrid work model?
4. Suggest tools or practices to ensure accountability and monitor performance in remote teams.

• • •

Employee Engagement During Organizational Change

- **Background**

Alpha Motors, a leading automobile manufacturer, is undergoing a major organizational restructuring to remain competitive in the electric vehicle market. The restructuring involves merging departments, streamlining operations, and introducing new technologies. While necessary, these changes have led to uncertainty and anxiety among employees. A recent survey revealed that employee engagement has dropped by 25% since the announcement of the restructuring.

- **The Problem**

The HR department is tasked with ensuring a smooth transition while maintaining employee morale and engagement. Proposed initiatives include regular town hall meetings, a dedicated support team to address employee concerns, and training programs to upskill employees for new roles. However, there are concerns about whether these measures will be sufficient to address the underlying anxiety.

- **Key Questions:**

1. How can Alpha Motors maintain employee engagement during periods of significant change?
2. What role does transparent communication play in managing organizational change?
3. How can the company support employees in adapting to new roles and technologies?
4. Suggest additional strategies to minimize resistance to change.

• • •

Leadership Development in Family-Owned Businesses

- **Background**

Chowdhury Textiles, a family-owned business, has been a market leader in the textile industry for over five decades. However, as the business expands, there is a growing need for professional leadership. Currently, key leadership positions are held by family members, some of whom lack formal training in management. Employees have expressed concerns about limited opportunities for career growth and decision-making processes dominated by familial interests.

- **The Problem**

The company's HR team has suggested launching a leadership development program to identify and groom future leaders, both from within the family and the broader workforce. However, there is resistance from senior family members who fear losing control over the business.

- **Key Questions:**

1. What challenges are unique to leadership development in family-owned businesses?
2. How can Chowdhury Textiles balance family interests with the need for professional leadership?
3. What elements should be included in the leadership development program to ensure its success?
4. How can the company address employee concerns about limited career growth opportunities?

• • •

Addressing Workplace Burnout

- **Background**

NovaCare, a leading healthcare provider, has seen a rise in employee burnout over the past year. Long working hours, high patient loads, and emotional stress have significantly impacted the well-being of healthcare professionals. A recent report indicated that 40% of employees feel exhausted, and 30% are considering leaving the organization.

- **The Problem**

The HR team has proposed several measures to address burnout, including hiring additional staff, offering mental health resources, and introducing mandatory wellness breaks. However, implementing these measures comes with challenges, such as budget constraints and ensuring that patient care standards are not compromised.

Key Questions:

1. What are the primary causes of workplace burnout, and how can NovaCare address them effectively?
2. How can the organization ensure that employee well-being initiatives do not compromise patient care?
3. What role does organizational culture play in preventing burnout?
4. Suggest cost-effective strategies to support employee mental health and well-being.

• • •

FINANCE

Corporate Governance and Financial Scandals

- **Case Overview**

In 2001, the global financial world was shaken by one of the largest corporate frauds in history: the Enron scandal. Enron Corporation, an American energy company, was considered a giant in its industry, boasting an innovative and fast-growing business model. However, behind this facade of success, the company employed questionable accounting practices to conceal its financial losses. These practices involved creating special purpose entities (SPEs) to hide debt and inflate profits artificially.

The key figures in the scandal included Enron's CEO Jeffrey Skilling and CFO Andrew Fastow, who orchestrated the fraudulent schemes. They used mark-to-market accounting, a practice that allowed the company to book profits from long-term contracts immediately, even if these profits were uncertain. This created a misleading picture of financial stability, which attracted investors and kept Enron's stock prices high.

The downfall of Enron began when financial analysts and investigative journalists started questioning its complex financial structures. The U.S. Securities and Exchange Commission (SEC) launched an investigation, revealing widespread fraud. Enron's stock prices plummeted, and the company declared bankruptcy in December 2001, wiping out shareholder value and employee pensions.

The Enron scandal highlighted severe lapses in corporate governance, ethics, and the oversight mechanisms of auditing firms. Arthur Andersen, Enron's auditor, was found complicit in the fraud for shredding critical documents and faced criminal charges, leading to the firm's dissolution.

- **Discussion Questions:**

1. How did poor corporate governance contribute to the Enron scandal?
2. What role did auditors play in the downfall of Enron, and how can auditor independence be ensured?

3. Discuss the impact of financial scandals like Enron on investor confidence.
4. Suggest measures to prevent similar corporate governance failures in the future.

• • •

Financial Risk Management in the Banking Sector

- **Case Overview**

The 2008 global financial crisis revealed the significance of robust financial risk management practices. One of the most affected institutions during this period was Lehman Brothers, a global financial services firm. Lehman Brothers' collapse was primarily attributed to its excessive exposure to subprime mortgages and an over-reliance on short-term funding.

Lehman Brothers aggressively pursued high-risk investments in mortgage-backed securities (MBS) and collateralized debt obligations (CDOs). As housing prices declined, the value of these assets plummeted, leading to massive losses. Simultaneously, the firm's reliance on repo agreements—short-term loans secured by collateral—made it vulnerable to liquidity crises. When counterparties refused to roll over these loans, Lehman Brothers was unable to meet its obligations.

The lack of proper risk management frameworks and inadequate stress testing worsened the situation. Lehman Brothers' executives underestimated the systemic risks posed by the housing bubble and failed to diversify their investment portfolio. Despite government efforts to stabilize the financial sector, Lehman Brothers filed for bankruptcy in September 2008, marking the largest bankruptcy filing in U.S. history.

The crisis underscored the importance of effective risk management, including credit risk, market risk, and liquidity risk. Post-crisis, regulatory bodies introduced stricter norms, such as Basel III, to strengthen the banking sector's resilience.

- **Discussion Questions:**

1. What were the primary risk management failures that led to Lehman Brothers' collapse?

2. How did the global financial crisis reshape risk management practices in the banking industry?
3. Evaluate the effectiveness of Basel III in addressing systemic risks.
4. What lessons can financial institutions learn from Lehman Brothers' experience?

• • •

CHAPTER CV

Venture Capital Financing and Startups

- **Case Overview**

In 2014, Flipkart, an Indian e-commerce giant, secured $1 billion in funding from venture capitalists (VCs). This marked one of the largest funding rounds for an Indian startup at the time. Flipkart's business model focused on online retail, leveraging India's growing internet penetration and digital payments ecosystem. The funding enabled Flipkart to compete aggressively with global rivals like Amazon.

Venture capitalists were attracted to Flipkart's potential for exponential growth. The funding was utilized to scale operations, improve supply chain infrastructure, and enhance customer experience. Flipkart also introduced innovative features such as cash-on-delivery and easy returns, which resonated with Indian consumers.

Despite its success, Flipkart faced challenges in managing profitability and operational costs. The heavy discounts offered to attract customers strained its finances. Moreover, the intense competition in the e-commerce space forced Flipkart to continually innovate and invest in technology.

The story of Flipkart underscores the critical role of VCs in fueling startup growth. However, it also highlights the challenges of balancing growth and profitability in a competitive market.

- **Discussion Questions:**

1. What factors made Flipkart an attractive investment for venture capitalists?
2. How did Flipkart manage to differentiate itself in a competitive e-commerce market?
3. Discuss the challenges faced by startups in achieving profitability while scaling operations.
4. How can startups balance investor expectations and long-term sustainability?

• • •

154

Mergers and Acquisitions in the Banking Industry

- **Case Overview**

The merger of State Bank of India (SBI) with its five associate banks in 2017 was a landmark event in the Indian banking sector. The merger aimed to consolidate SBI's position as a global banking giant and improve operational efficiencies. The associate banks included State Bank of Bikaner & Jaipur, State Bank of Patiala, and others.

The consolidation brought significant benefits, such as a larger capital base, improved credit capacity, and a unified brand image. However, the merger also posed challenges, including cultural integration, rationalization of branches, and employee concerns.

Post-merger, SBI's market share increased, making it one of the top 50 global banks. The bank leveraged its enhanced scale to offer competitive interest rates and expand its digital banking services. Despite initial hiccups, the merger was considered a success, setting a precedent for future consolidations in the Indian banking sector.

- **Discussion Questions:**

1. What were the strategic benefits of SBI's merger with its associate banks?
2. Discuss the challenges faced during the integration process.
3. How did the merger impact SBI's financial performance and market position?
4. What lessons can other banks learn from SBI's consolidation experience?

• • •

Cryptocurrency and Financial Regulations

- **Case Overview**

Bitcoin, the first cryptocurrency, gained global attention after its meteoric rise in value in 2017. This decentralized digital currency operates on blockchain technology, eliminating the need for intermediaries like banks. While cryptocurrencies offer benefits such as transparency and lower transaction costs, they also pose risks, including volatility, fraud, and regulatory challenges.

In India, the regulatory environment for cryptocurrencies has been uncertain. The Reserve Bank of India (RBI) initially prohibited banks from dealing with crypto-related transactions in 2018, citing risks to financial stability. However, the Supreme Court lifted this ban in 2020, enabling cryptocurrency exchanges to operate legally.

Despite regulatory clarity, the adoption of cryptocurrencies remains limited due to concerns about security and the lack of consumer awareness. Governments worldwide are exploring the potential of Central Bank Digital Currencies (CBDCs) as an alternative to private cryptocurrencies. India's Digital Rupee initiative represents a step in this direction, aiming to combine the benefits of digital currencies with the stability of fiat money.

Discussion Questions:

1. What are the potential benefits and risks of cryptocurrencies for financial markets?
2. Discuss the impact of regulatory uncertainty on cryptocurrency adoption in India.
3. How can governments balance innovation and regulation in the cryptocurrency space?
4. Compare the features of cryptocurrencies and Central Bank Digital Currencies (CBDCs).

• • •

Financial Inclusion through Microfinance

- **Case Overview**

Grameen Bank, founded by Muhammad Yunus in Bangladesh, revolutionized financial inclusion through microfinance. The bank provided small, collateral-free loans to low-income individuals, particularly women, enabling them to start small businesses and improve their livelihoods.

The microfinance model leveraged group lending, where borrowers formed groups to ensure mutual accountability. This approach minimized default rates and fostered community development. Grameen Bank's success inspired similar initiatives globally, including India's Self-Help Group (SHG) model.

However, the microfinance sector has faced criticism for high-interest rates and aggressive recovery practices. In India, the Andhra Pradesh microfinance crisis in 2010 highlighted the need for regulatory oversight. The crisis resulted from over-indebtedness and unethical practices by some microfinance institutions (MFIs).

Despite challenges, microfinance remains a powerful tool for poverty alleviation and financial inclusion. The introduction of digital technology has further enhanced the sector's reach and efficiency.

- **Discussion Questions:**

1. How has microfinance contributed to financial inclusion in developing countries?
2. Discuss the challenges faced by the microfinance sector and potential solutions.
3. Evaluate the role of technology in transforming microfinance operations.

• • •

Capital Budgeting at TechWave Inc.

- **Background:**

TechWave Inc., a rapidly growing tech startup, specializes in developing artificial intelligence-based software for businesses. The company has recently developed a new product that is projected to significantly impact the marketplace. However, before moving forward, TechWave's management needs to decide whether to invest in the project. The company has to evaluate the potential returns and risks associated with the project, and decide if the investment is worth pursuing.

- **Challenges:**

TechWave has a limited budget, and the company's CFO, Sarah Williams, is considering using capital budgeting techniques to evaluate the project. She is particularly focused on Net Present Value (NPV), Internal Rate of Return (IRR), and Payback Period methods. The CFO is concerned about the project's cash flow, especially in the early stages. Additionally, the company is considering taking on a loan to finance the project, which would increase the financial risk.

- **Details:**

The product development will require an initial investment of $500,000. TechWave expects the project to generate the following cash flows over the next five years:

- Year 1: $100,000
- Year 2: $120,000
- Year 3: $150,000
- Year 4: $180,000
- Year 5: $200,000

TechWave's cost of capital is 10%, and the company has a target payback period of 4 years. The CFO also wants to know the IRR for the project to assess its profitability.

- **Analysis Tools:**

1. **Net Present Value (NPV):** Discounting the future cash flows at the company's cost of capital of 10%.
2. **Internal Rate of Return (IRR):** Finding the rate at which the NPV of the project becomes zero.
3. **Payback Period:** Calculating how long it will take to recover the initial investment.

- **Decision-Making:** Sarah is faced with the critical task of using these financial tools to determine if the project is financially viable. She must also consider the impact of financing options such as loans or issuing new equity, as this would influence the cost of capital and the overall risk profile of the company.

- **Questions for Discussion:**

1. Based on the NPV, IRR, and Payback Period, should TechWave go ahead with the project? Why or why not?
2. What are the limitations of using these capital budgeting techniques in this case?
3. How would the financing method (debt or equity) affect the company's decision-making process?
4. What are the risks associated with not taking the project forward, and how can they be mitigated?

• • •

Working Capital Management at Stellar Foods Ltd.

- **Background:**

Stellar Foods Ltd. is a leading manufacturer and distributor of packaged snacks. The company has experienced significant growth over the last few years but is now facing liquidity issues. Despite the increase in sales, Stellar Foods is struggling with cash flow management and inventory turnover. As a result, the company is finding it difficult to pay its suppliers and meet short-term obligations.

- **Challenges:**

The CFO of Stellar Foods, Rajeev Sharma, has identified that the company's working capital management practices need immediate improvement. The company has a high inventory turnover rate, but the average collection period for receivables is increasing, and the payable period has shortened. Additionally, the company is facing pressure from suppliers for timely payments.

- **Details:**

The company's current assets and liabilities are as follows:

- **Current Assets:**

  - Cash: $150,000
  - Accounts Receivable: $400,000
  - Inventory: $500,000

- **Current Liabilities:**

- ◦ Accounts Payable: $300,000
- ◦ Short-term loans: $100,000

Rajeev has asked his finance team to analyze the company's cash conversion cycle and recommend ways to improve the liquidity position. They are also considering renegotiating supplier terms and improving receivables collection.

- **Analysis Tools:**

1. **Cash Conversion Cycle (CCC):** Calculate the average time it takes for the company to convert its investments in inventory and receivables into cash.
2. **Receivables Turnover:** Analyzing how efficiently the company collects payments from customers.
3. **Inventory Turnover:** Assessing the efficiency of inventory management.
4. **Payables Turnover:** Examining how quickly the company pays its suppliers.

- **Decision-Making:**

Rajeev is faced with multiple decisions, such as improving working capital efficiency by speeding up receivables collection and extending payables terms. He must also consider the implications of these changes on relationships with customers and suppliers.

- **Questions for Discussion:**

1. How can Stellar Foods improve its working capital management to resolve its liquidity issues?
2. What strategies should the company consider for reducing the cash conversion cycle?
3. How would improving receivables and inventory turnover affect the company's liquidity and profitability?
4. What risks might Stellar Foods face if they extend payment terms with suppliers?

• • •

Financial Risk Management at Global Tech Co.

- **Background:**

Global Tech Co. is a multinational technology firm with operations in the US, Europe, and Asia. The company is concerned about the exposure to currency risk due to its international operations. A significant portion of its revenues comes from Europe, and the company has been experiencing fluctuations in the exchange rates between the US Dollar and the Euro.

- **Challenges:**

The CFO, Mary Stevens, has been tasked with assessing the currency risk exposure and deciding whether to use hedging techniques to mitigate the risks. The company has two options: enter into forward contracts to lock in exchange rates, or use options to provide more flexibility.

- **Details:**

Global Tech Co.'s revenues from Europe amount to €10 million per year, and the company is worried about the Euro depreciating against the US Dollar, which would reduce the dollar value of European revenues. Currently, the exchange rate is 1 USD = 0.90 EUR, but it could fall to 1 USD = 0.85 EUR. The company is considering using a forward contract to hedge its future revenue flows.

- **Analysis Tools:**

1. **Forward Contract**: Locking in an exchange rate for future transactions.
2. **Currency Options**: Purchasing options to hedge against unfavorable exchange rate movements while maintaining the opportunity to benefit from favorable movements.
3. **Risk Analysis**: Assessing the impact of currency fluctuations on the company's financial performance.

- **Decision-Making:** Mary must weigh the pros and cons of forward contracts versus currency options, considering the company's risk tolerance, the potential costs, and the expected currency fluctuations.
- **Questions for Discussion:**

1. What are the advantages and disadvantages of using forward contracts to hedge currency risk?
2. How do currency options differ from forward contracts in terms of risk management?
3. How should Mary assess the company's risk exposure and decide on the best hedging strategy?
4. What impact might currency fluctuations have on Global Tech's profitability and competitive position?

• • •

Dividend Policy Decision at Summit Enterprises

- **Background:**

Summit Enterprises is a mid-sized manufacturing company that has been steadily growing its revenue and profits. The company's management is debating whether to increase the dividend payout to its shareholders or reinvest the profits back into the business for expansion. The company has a strong cash flow but is also eyeing several strategic investments.

- **Challenges:**

The CEO, James Thompson, has asked the finance team to evaluate the company's dividend policy. The company's shareholders are asking for a higher dividend, but the management team believes that reinvestment will generate higher returns in the long term.

- **Details:**

Summit Enterprises currently pays a dividend of $1.50 per share. The company's earnings per share (EPS) for the last year was $4.00. The company is considering whether to increase the dividend by 50% or retain more earnings to fund an expansion plan, which is expected to require an investment of $3 million.

- **Analysis Tools:**

1. **Dividend Payout Ratio**: Calculating the percentage of earnings paid out as dividends.
2. **Retention Ratio**: Determining how much of the company's earnings are retained for reinvestment.
3. **Growth Potential**: Assessing the potential returns from reinvested earnings versus immediate dividend payouts.

- **Decision-Making:**

James must decide whether to maintain or increase the dividend payout, considering the company's growth opportunities and the preferences of the shareholders.

- **Questions for Discussion:**

1. How would increasing the dividend payout affect Summit Enterprises' future growth prospects?
2. Should Summit Enterprises prioritize shareholder dividends or reinvest profits for business expansion?
3. What is the impact of a high dividend payout ratio on the company's financial flexibility?
4. How should James balance the needs of shareholders with the long-term goals of the company?

• • •

Mergers and Acquisitions Strategy at Apex Pharmaceuticals

- **Background:**

Apex Pharmaceuticals, a leading player in the generic drug market, is considering acquiring a smaller rival, MedicoPharm, to expand its product line and gain market share. Apex has a strong cash reserve but is contemplating whether to finance the acquisition through cash or debt.

- **Challenges:**

Apex's management team, led by CEO Robert Green, needs to assess the strategic fit of MedicoPharm and determine whether the acquisition would provide value to shareholders. The company must also decide on the method of financing, as this will impact its financial stability and cost of capital.

- **Details:**

MedicoPharm has a market capitalization of $100 million, and Apex is offering $120 million for the acquisition. Apex has $60 million in cash reserves and is considering issuing bonds to finance the rest of the acquisition cost.

- **Analysis Tools:**

1. **Valuation Methods:** Using discounted cash flow (DCF) analysis and comparable company analysis to value MedicoPharm.
2. **Synergies:** Assessing the potential synergies from the acquisition, such as cost savings and revenue growth.
3. **Financing Options:** Analyzing the pros and cons of financing the acquisition through cash reserves versus debt.

- **Decision-Making:**

Robert needs to evaluate whether the acquisition will add shareholder value and how the financing decision will affect the company's future performance and risk profile.

- **Questions for Discussion:**

1. What are the key factors to consider when evaluating a potential acquisition?
2. How should Apex assess the potential synergies from the acquisition of MedicoPharm?
3. What are the advantages and disadvantages of financing the acquisition with debt versus cash?
4. How would the acquisition affect Apex's financial position and shareholder value?

• • •

Financial Planning and Forecasting at Innovate Corp.

- **Background:**

Innovate Corp. is a technology firm specializing in software development. The company has experienced rapid growth, but the management team is concerned about potential fluctuations in cash flow due to high fixed costs. The CFO, Emily Jackson, has been tasked with preparing a financial forecast for the next three years and creating a plan for sustainable growth.

- **Challenges:**

Emily must prepare a comprehensive financial forecast that will guide the company's budget decisions. She needs to account for expected revenue growth, potential cost increases, and the possibility of market downturns. Additionally, she must evaluate the company's capital structure and financing needs.

- **Details:**

Innovate Corp. has projected a 10% increase in revenue year-over-year, but the company's fixed costs are also expected to rise by 5% annually. The company is considering taking on additional debt to fund research and development (R&D) efforts.

- **Analysis Tools:**

1. **Financial Forecasting:** Projecting income statements, balance sheets, and cash flows.
2. **Break-even Analysis:** Calculating the sales volume required to cover fixed and variable costs.

3. **Capital Structure**: Analyzing the mix of debt and equity financing.

- **Decision-Making:**

Emily must decide on the best way to balance growth with financial stability, and she must present a strategy for managing the company's cash flow and financing needs.

Questions for Discussion:

1. What are the key components of a comprehensive financial forecast?
2. How should Innovate Corp. plan for potential downturns in the market?
3. What impact will additional debt have on the company's financial stability?
4. How can Innovate Corp. balance sustainable growth with the need to maintain positive cash flow?

• • •

Financial Decision-Making in Startups

- **Background:**

A fintech startup, FinGrow, was founded in 2019 with the vision of simplifying personal financial management for millennials. The company quickly attracted venture capital (VC) funding due to its innovative app that offered budget planning, investment tracking, and personalized financial advice. By the end of 2021, FinGrow had raised $15 million in VC funding and achieved a user base of 1 million. However, as it planned to expand into new markets and launch premium features, the company faced critical financial decisions.

- **Challenge**
  FinGrow's management team needed to allocate their funds strategically to maximize growth while ensuring financial sustainability. Key areas under consideration included:

1. **Product Development**: Investing $5 million to enhance the app's artificial intelligence capabilities and user interface.
2. **Marketing**: Allocating $3 million for a targeted campaign to expand its user base in the U.S. and Canada.
3. **International Expansion**: Using $4 million to establish operations in Europe and Asia.
4. **Operational Costs**: Setting aside $2 million for hiring, infrastructure, and legal compliance.

Each decision carried its own risks and opportunities. For instance, investing heavily in product development might delay profitability but could increase the app's competitive edge. Conversely, prioritizing international expansion could result in rapid growth but expose the company to market-specific risks and cultural challenges.

- **Decision and Outcome:**

After intense deliberation, FinGrow's management decided to prioritize product development and marketing while delaying international expansion. The rationale was to solidify their market position and improve customer retention before entering new territories. The $8 million allocation was divided as follows:

- $5 million for product development
- $3 million for marketing

The remaining $7 million was reserved for operational costs and unforeseen contingencies.

By mid-2023, FinGrow's user base grew to 3 million, and its premium subscription model generated a monthly revenue of $2 million. Despite the initial hesitation, the decision to delay international expansion was deemed successful as it allowed the company to build a robust product and a loyal customer base.

- **Questions**

1. What factors should FinGrow consider when deciding on future international expansion?
2. How can the company balance growth and financial sustainability?
3. What are the potential risks of delaying international expansion for a startup like FinGrow?
4. Evaluate the importance of VC funding in FinGrow's early growth.
5. Suggest alternative strategies FinGrow could have used to allocate its funds.

• • •

Corporate Restructuring at a Manufacturing Firm

- **Background:**

SteelCore, a mid-sized manufacturing company specializing in industrial equipment, faced declining profits due to increasing competition and rising raw material costs. In 2020, the company reported a 15% drop in revenue, prompting the board to initiate a corporate restructuring plan. The primary goal was to streamline operations and reduce costs while maintaining market share.

- **Challenge:**

The restructuring plan included:

1. **Downsizing**: Reducing the workforce by 20% to cut labor costs.
2. **Divestment**: Selling underperforming business units that contributed only 5% to the company's revenue but accounted for 15% of operational expenses.
3. **Automation**: Investing $10 million in advanced manufacturing technologies to improve efficiency.
4. **Debt Restructuring**: Negotiating with creditors to extend loan repayment timelines and reduce interest rates.

However, these measures posed significant challenges. Downsizing risked damaging employee morale, and divestment could hurt long-term growth potential. Moreover, the $10 million investment in automation required upfront capital, putting additional strain on the company's finances.

- **Decision and Outcome:**

SteelCore's management implemented the restructuring plan in phases. They started with the divestment of two underperforming units, which generated $25 million in cash. This was followed by the automation initiative, funded partly by the proceeds from divestment and partly through a new loan with favorable terms.

By 2023, SteelCore achieved a 30% increase in operational efficiency and a 10% rise in profit margins. Employee morale improved over time due to transparent communication and retraining programs for those affected by downsizing. The restructuring helped SteelCore regain its competitive edge in the market.

- **Questions:**

1. Analyze the role of automation in improving SteelCore's operational efficiency.
2. Discuss the ethical considerations involved in workforce downsizing.
3. How can divestment impact a company's long-term growth strategy?
4. Evaluate the importance of debt restructuring in SteelCore's recovery.
5. Suggest additional measures that SteelCore could adopt to maintain profitability.

• • •

Risk Management in Banking

- **Background:**

Global Bank, a multinational financial institution, faced a significant challenge in 2022 when interest rate fluctuations and market volatility led to increased credit defaults. The bank's exposure to risky loans, particularly in emerging markets, raised concerns among stakeholders about its risk management practices.

- **Challenge:**

To address the issue, Global Bank's risk management team proposed the following measures:

1. **Portfolio Diversification:** Reducing exposure to high-risk loans by diversifying into more stable sectors such as renewable energy and infrastructure.
2. **Improved Credit Screening:** Enhancing credit assessment models using AI to predict borrower default risks more accurately.
3. **Hedging Strategies:** Implementing financial derivatives to hedge against interest rate and currency risks.
4. **Stress Testing:** Conducting regular stress tests to evaluate the bank's resilience under adverse economic scenarios.

Implementing these measures required significant investment in technology and expertise. Additionally, shifting the loan portfolio posed challenges as it involved realigning relationships with long-standing clients in high-risk sectors.

- **Decision and Outcome**

The bank prioritized improved credit screening and stress testing, investing $20 million in AI tools and hiring risk management experts.

Portfolio diversification was initiated gradually, with a focus on sectors offering steady returns. Hedging strategies were implemented to mitigate immediate risks from volatile interest rates.

By 2024, Global Bank reduced its non-performing assets by 25% and improved its capital adequacy ratio. Stakeholder confidence was restored, and the bank's stock price increased by 15%.

- **Questions**

1. How can AI enhance credit screening processes in the banking industry?
2. Discuss the importance of stress testing in risk management.
3. What challenges can arise from diversifying a loan portfolio?
4. Evaluate the effectiveness of hedging strategies in mitigating financial risks.
5. Propose additional measures Global Bank could adopt to strengthen its risk management framework.

• • •

Capital Budgeting in Healthcare

- **Background:**

MediHealth, a regional healthcare provider, planned to build a new state-of-the-art facility to address increasing patient demand. The project, estimated to cost $50 million, included advanced diagnostic equipment, modern surgical units, and a dedicated research wing. MediHealth's leadership faced a critical capital budgeting decision: how to finance the project and ensure its profitability.

- **Challenge**

The management team considered three financing options:

1. **Equity Financing**: Raising funds by issuing new shares, potentially diluting existing ownership but avoiding debt.
2. **Debt Financing**: Securing a long-term loan with an interest rate of 7% annually, which would increase financial leverage.
3. **Public-Private Partnership (PPP)**: Partnering with government agencies and private investors to share costs and risks.

Additionally, MediHealth conducted a feasibility study to project the facility's cash flows over the next 10 years. Key considerations included:

- An expected increase in patient volume by 30% annually.
- Rising operational costs due to higher staffing needs.
- Potential competition from nearby healthcare providers.

- **Decision and Outcome:**

After evaluating the options, MediHealth opted for a hybrid approach, combining debt financing and PPP. They secured a $30 million loan and partnered with a private investor to cover the remaining $20 million. The project was completed in 2023, ahead of schedule.

In its first year, the new facility contributed a 20% increase in MediHealth's overall revenue. While operational costs rose, the facility's efficiency and patient satisfaction led to long-term profitability.

- **Questions**

1. What factors should MediHealth consider when choosing between equity and debt financing?
2. Discuss the advantages and disadvantages of public-private partnerships in healthcare projects.
3. How can MediHealth mitigate the risks associated with rising operational costs?
4. Evaluate the role of feasibility studies in capital budgeting decisions.
5. Suggest strategies to ensure the long-term profitability of MediHealth's new facility.

• • •

Ethical Investing at an Asset Management Firm

- **Background**

GreenInvest, an asset management firm, specialized in socially responsible and ethical investments. By 2021, the firm's assets under management (AUM) reached $5 billion, driven by growing demand for environmental, social, and governance (ESG) investments. However, GreenInvest faced criticism when an investigation revealed that some of its portfolio companies had questionable labor practices and environmental violations.

- **Challenge:**

To restore its reputation, GreenInvest's leadership implemented the following measures:

1. **Enhanced Screening**: Adopting stricter ESG criteria to evaluate potential investments.
2. **Active Engagement**: Collaborating with portfolio companies to improve their ESG practices.
3. **Transparency**: Publishing detailed ESG impact reports to maintain stakeholder trust.
4. **Divestment**: Exiting investments in companies that failed to meet ESG standards.

These actions required additional resources and posed the risk of reduced short-term returns. However, maintaining the firm's ethical commitment was crucial for retaining clients and attracting new investors.

- **Decision and Outcome:**

GreenInvest enhanced its screening process using AI tools and dedicated a team to monitor ESG compliance. By 2023, the firm divested from 10 non-compliant companies and partnered with several organizations to promote sustainable practices. The firm's AUM grew to $7 billion, reflecting increased client trust.

- **Questions**

1. How can asset managers balance profitability with ethical investing principles?
2. Discuss the challenges of implementing stricter ESG criteria in investment decisions.
3. Evaluate the importance of transparency in maintaining stakeholder trust.
4. What are the potential risks and rewards of divesting from non-compliant companies?
5. Propose additional measures GreenInvest could take to enhance its ESG practices.

• • •

Cost Control in Retail

- **Background:**

TrendMart, a leading retail chain, faced declining profit margins due to rising supply chain costs and increased competition from e-commerce platforms. In 2021, the company launched a cost control initiative aimed at improving profitability without compromising customer experience.

- **Challenge:**

The initiative focused on three key areas:

1. **Supply Chain Optimization**: Partnering with local suppliers to reduce transportation costs and minimize delivery times.
2. **Inventory Management**: Implementing advanced analytics to optimize stock levels and reduce overstocking.
3. **Operational Efficiency**: Reducing energy consumption in stores and adopting self-checkout systems to lower labor costs.

While these measures offered significant cost-saving potential, they also involved substantial initial investments and required employee training. Additionally, TrendMart risked alienating customers if changes disrupted their shopping experience.

- **Decision and Outcome:**

TrendMart invested $15 million in analytics software and infrastructure upgrades. They also launched a pilot program to test self-checkout systems in select stores. By 2023, the company reduced supply chain costs by 20% and improved inventory turnover by 15%. Customer satisfaction surveys indicated minimal disruption, and the initiative's success was expanded chain-wide.

- **Questions:**

1. Analyze the role of analytics in optimizing inventory management.
2. Discuss the potential challenges of implementing self-checkout systems in retail.
3. How can TrendMart ensure customer satisfaction while controlling costs?
4. Evaluate the importance of supply chain partnerships in cost control.
5. Suggest additional strategies TrendMart could adopt to maintain profitability.

• • •